My Betfan Year

Following the ups and downs of Britain's leading tipster and pro-gambler

By Andrew Bell

To join Andy Bell's Betfan horseracing tipster service,

visit: andybellbetfan.com/ab

Or the Late Call Betting Service: andybellbetfan.com/lc

First published 2014

ISBN 978-1505386295

Urban Media Publishing Ltd,
1-5 The Shambles,
York YO1 7LZ.
Web: urbanmediapublishing.co.uk

Introduction

It's often said Britain is a nation of shopkeepers, well it may be but it's also a nation of gamblers and this book is written by one of the greatest of them all - Andrew Bell.

I had been on the trail of 'Bellie Boy' for several years and 18 months ago I brought him to Betfan where in Andy Bell Racing he has produced one of the greatest tipping services ever seen and a constantly growing happy band of members.

It wasn't an accident, I was on Bellie Boy's trail, stories of him being the original rock 'n' roll tipster/on course player were known from Lands' End to Wallsend and also was the belief that behind the jokey exterior and owners' bar aficionado was a ruthless and calculated operator.

In my view, Andy Bell is an old school yet thoroughly modern operator, that's what makes him so fascinating and so successful. He is on course often and utilises all of its plus points yet he is active on the exchanges and is a keen student of times and ratings.

This book will take you inside his world in a deeper way than his Betfan diary ever could and provide you with vital advice that will help you in your battle to slay the bookmaker and it will also make you laugh out loud many times.

I'm often asked, "What is Bellie really like - is it as he comes across in the diary?" The answer is always a resounding "Yes!"

What you see is what you get and though he doesn't suffer fools there's no malice in him.

This guy gets invited behind the locked doors at the heart of racing and he will take you behind those doors with him in this book, so get ready, enjoy and if you're ever out at the races and you hear a Norfolk/Suffolk accent offering an opinion, if he looks like Rick Parfitt after a hard night - you would be very wise to listen!

Simon Holden

Fellow Betfan tipster

Chapter One

My career with Betfan begins

Having been a professional gambler for many years now, the decision to come out of the shadows has been a difficult one. I have used my experience and tactical nous to develop a winning combination when it comes to backing a horse to win and I'm willing to share that knowledge with race fans on the Betfan website. For those who don't know, Betfan is a premier platform of some of the best sports tipsters in the UK - so when I got the call I was honoured to be involved.

Obviously, it also opened another source of income for me but it also allows me to express an opinion on the state of racing in this country - something I am truly passionate about. I realise that I live a life many people can only dream about and I go to several racecourses every week and, usually, end up leaving each one with a lot more cash than when I went in.

However, the column I write every week and the tips I offer most days also give me a chance to show that there is a great deal of work, travel and socialising involved in turning punting into a profitable past time.

It's not impossible for others to follow in my footsteps

and I will be offering help in choosing winning horses and reveal some of my own expertise too. Even if you don't want to make a nice side-line earning what is free money, I hope this book is as enjoyable for race fans and non-race fans alike.

So to work: after a big build-up I have quite a sizeable number of clients to my tipping service and I'm at Yarmouth but there are no tips to give. Micky Quinn landed a 20/1 winner, which made him dance in the ring afterwards, but I get talking to three trainers about their horses and I learn some very interesting information.

There are a couple of things to realise before we go any further: backing race horses is not a 'quick-fix' solution to earning money - it's a job like any other that you have to apply yourself to. This means that you should forget a great winning day, put a poor day behind you, and count up how much you have made over the month. This is the only way to beat the inevitable poor runs and losses that come with the job.

The second thing to remember is that you can't just sit down and read all the published information about a horse - you need to get out there and see them in action, make notes of horses with potential, learn what to look for, where does the horse like running, what conditions suit?

The list is endless but with time you will pick up the

nuances of what professionals actually look for.

Allied to this is the 'socialising'. Yes, we all enjoy going racing and having a few beers but for many it's a 'day at the office' and you are there to work - enjoy a pint but have fun afterwards. Get into the best enclosure or where the owners and trainers congregate and get to know these people. They like to talk, they like to have a laugh so be friendly and outgoing and you will learn more doing this than what you could ever do by studying the form in a newspaper.

However, this also means getting up at the crack of dawn and going to watch the horses in action on the gallops - the one at Newmarket is a hotbed of information and gossip. I'm well-known to those who work in HQ's yards and they are happy to speak with me. I'm happy treating them to a beer whenever I see them at a racecourse in return!

Oh, and when you sign up for a prestigious tipping service, such as one run by Betfan, then the pressure is really on - especially when your advice is to go out in ten minutes and you have nothing, literally nothing, to give on a big day's racing then you will know what pressure really is.

So, to my new career. I went to Yarmouth for a depressing eight race card with small fields in each. My first tip was each way which started at 11s and was punted into 7s and, inevitably, rolled in fourth. My next at Brighton came second.

The following day I was at Newmarket and I set off early to beat the crowds, it's one of those music events that I quite enjoy which pull in punters who wouldn't otherwise go horse racing.

I had my first Betfan winner for a four points win and then decide it's easier to find winners than it is to get a beer. It's just as well since the gents are crammed with women and I consider making a small fortune selling 'Shewees' at these big race events.

Then it's onto Saturday. I'll be honest here - Saturdays are not my favourite betting day. This is because I'm looking for profits and it's the hardest day of the week to find winners when everyone wants to bet. I went to Newmarket and after racking up three losers and my mobile is busier a bookies' satchel with calls and texts. Not all of them complimentary. But do you know, I got beaten in three races by two 33/1 winners and a 25/1 shot - how anyone can find those priced winners consistently is beyond me.

The good news is that I made a profit over the week - albeit a small one but I still made money. My debut on that Saturday in early August 2013, after a week of fanfare and a huge build-up, saw my first tips go disastrously wrong. To say I was gutted about the results would be an understatement but that's just horseracing. No-one can predict a winner in every single race but the following day I publish my first column which goes out to more than 30,000 subscribers and I'm honest enough to own up to a hesitant start.

I was on a downer after my dismal showing on my 1st Saturday with Betfan (as you are all well aware) so I was wary about throwing too many points around with gay abandon. From 8am the mobile started ringing and bleeping (immediately I was thinking this is the local lads after having a count up and grumpy with their hangovers and thinking Grrr "ANDY BELL") but it was a constant flow of information which continued until around 11am.

And this is the real secret to successful punting on horse races; everyone has a bad day and the trick is to pick yourself up and carry on knowing that a good run is just ahead of you.

However, my second week of tipping is another run of disappointments. I broke all of my own rules to put up a horse called Beacon Lodge which had not run for two years but was starting at even money. It came as no surprise to watch it drift like a barge and run like a drain to finish fourth.

My next tip was the Andrew Balding trained

Personnel which I put out at 11/2 each way and as it entered the final furlong I thought I was onto a winner only to see him veer towards the rails and blow his chance of winning, though I pick up a small return.

My third bet of the day was Colonel Mak, ridden by Paul Hanagan, which hit the front and never saw a horse in the entire race to win by four lengths. I tipped it 5/1 each way and it was then heavily backed into 100/30.

I must be honest here and confess that in my career I have backed thousands of winners but this particular win was very sweet and led to a good profit on the day and help restore my reputation. I had a very good night's sleep, mainly through relief.

The following day was an interesting one since overnight there was heavy rain and the going had been changed to heavy/soft in places and the one horse I was interested in doesn't travel well unless it is firm ground so I decided it was a no bet day at Ayr.

However, my contacts had flagged up a horse called Diplomat running in Galway, trained by Willie Mullins and ridden by Ruby Walsh which is usually a solid combination but I still carefully went through the form and tipped it to pick up a four-point win.

Unusually for me I opt not to travel to Glorious

Goodwood, the first time I've missed this meeting in six years and instead head towards Yarmouth. Again, I put up three bets but the first one which was running at Yarmouth is a horse I'm very fond of called Signo Sassi but heading to the start he unseated his rider, refused to enter the stalls and then fluffed the start by five lengths. I am a patient man so I wrote that I am only going to give him one more chance because I believe he has a lot of ability.

All professional gamblers have horses they follow and they are forever making notes in their notebook about which ones will eventually turn a corner and spring a surprise on the bookies.

My second bet was another second and my third was a horse called Shamar ridden by Ruby who fluffed the last hurdle and was beaten by a short distance. It was a very frustrating race considering that Shamar had beaten the winner by three lengths the last time they met.

One of the really great things about what I do is that I get to travel the country to enjoy horseracing and then to enjoy the pubs and restaurants of the nearby town. I always enjoy Great Yarmouth and have had some interesting nights out there. This particular night was very good and I was out with some friends who live in the area but other than encountering a very boisterous hen party it was a very quiet night for me indeed.

The following morning and I am still smarting over Ruby's overconfident ride but I go through the Goodwood card to find two really good bets; one is a horse that has been catching the proverbial pigeons on the Newmarket gallops and the other is from the all-conquering Hannon team.

The first bet didn't win - I was very angry and this is what I eventually wrote in my Betfan column:

Our 1st bet EXCESS KNOWLEDGE, I have had to rewrite this three times and tone it down every time: how can a professional jockey be so tactically inept letting a 33/1 shot block him in and drop the reins twice on a horse that stays, why not use its stamina in a slowly ran race (is William Buick really up to a TOP job, or is he just a good jockey, on certain tracks?).

I could go on forever, but hey we've all seen and witnessed it but now the hard bit, explain to "her indoors" that the same happened today as yesterday, a professional well paid sportsman 'cocked up'. Note to myself: Now take a brisk walk in the cooling rain!!!

The day is saved when the jockey Richard Hughes manages to impress on my second tip to win at 13/2 to make it a decent winning day. I write:

A good winning day 3 outta 4. My 1st full week with BETFAN, which could have been soooooooo much better, had a nose and a neck gone our way, no explaining to her indoors now, fickle things us gamblers all of a sudden everything is rosy, skies are blue and grass is green.

As I mentioned earlier, another aspect to being a professional gambler is that it's not all about studying form, travelling to race courses and enjoying a good day's racing before hitting the pubs afterwards. There is still a lot of legwork involved and I visit the gallops at Newmarket on a regular basis to see the horses being put through their paces and to chat with the stable boys and girls as well as trainers.

My visit on this particular morning led to some very good information coming my way that I will put to good use in the coming weeks.

My tips for Goodwood didn't do as well as I thought they should have done, of three bets all three came in very close second places. This is a really strange situation since I am effectively exposing myself to thousands of followers as a professional punter who knows what he's doing but the results aren't going my way. There's a certain amount of frustration kicking in now but I know that with perseverance the luck will change.

Unfortunately, my tips that Friday all failed to impress and then I really do need to find some winners though I am pleased to see the end of the Goodwood Festival. I'm not entirely sure how punter-friendly this course is, it is something of a specialist track which still underlines the pressure I am under in trying to find winners for my followers.

Onto a third week and the weather changes and my success changes with it. Everyone who follows horseracing realises that ground conditions are a vital part of finding winners.

On the Monday my Irish connections deliver several winners and then I see that William Haggis has sent a horse called Battalion to Ripon for a four horse maiden race and I can't believe that it's only even money. At home, this horse is working with well-rated stable mates and it went on to win the race by five lengths to deliver a four-point win.

The following day, I noticed that the very shrewd Ian Williams has placed his own horse Star Alliance in a winnable two mile race and booked the jockey Graham Lee to do the steering. I snapped at the opportunity of 7/4 to see that the heavens opened and the race was won in a time that was 16 seconds slower than would be expected.

On Wednesday I head back to Yarmouth and tip a

horse ridden by Frankie Dettori but he hasn't read the script and the horse doesn't do as well as I would have expected. The rest of the day delivers a variety of seconds and poor performances.

I usually enjoy my nights out with friends in Yarmouth but after the day's events at the racecourse I just can't summon the enthusiasm and have to make my excuses and return early to my hotel.

This is what I told my Betfan readers:

Fresh as a daisy, I decided a breakfast and a quiet read of the Racing Post was in order, so I wandered down Regent Road to "La Continental" and was met by a wave of racing banter from the table in the corner.

Richard the owner called me over (that's ANOTHER free breakfast), Acle car centre offer me a new car heheheh and the young Michael Bells apprentice LOUIS STEWARD's father are all in debate.

Obviously the chat was ALL horses and LOUIS, and in fairness to the young lad he had rode a cracker the day before on his boss's horse Lovesome, only to be beaten a very game short head by George Baker.

Louis was still to ride his 1st winner at Yarmouth I was told and he had a good ride in the last today on TEVEZ, the former

Barney Curley charge, but noticed it had won the previous night at Kempton.

The room was buzzing with the expectations of young Louis, but I was cooler as I thought it probably wouldn't run again today so didn't tip it up for that reason. I decided to pin my colours to HEY DUDE that afternoon at Haydock and VITAL EVIDENCE at Sandown that night.

HEY DUDE won very nicely (tipped up at 7/2) and now I am waiting for VITAL EVIDENCE as I also have a nice e/w double.

To my amazement TEVEZ is still a runner in the last at Yarmouth and normally I leave before the last to miss the traffic, but I have to watch Louis. He misses the break by design or not I don't know, so I start slowly walking to the car but TEVEZ is always just interested but comes under a very determined pump about half a mile out and to my amazement the old boy keeps responding to the "up and coming" apprentice's urgings and finally wins going away by 1+ lengths, a great ride and a 1st winner at Yarmouth for Louis Steward.

I am impressed even though I/we have missed a winner, a young lad going places. Vital Evidence hits a brick wall and blows out but a good winning day and a lot learned.

That night I head into the bright lights of Yarmouth for a really good night and the following day I write this:

Early to rise because I must pop into La Continental for the gossip before heading to Newmarket, as soon as I turn the corner in Regent road, the noise hits me, a bus load of holiday makers?

No, just the racing table in the corner in full vocal swing and counting their 10/1ish Tevez gains. After a bout of told you so's, why didn't you back it, and lots of high spirits I refuse another foc breakfast and finding out Louis already has an agent make my lame excuses again and head to HQ.

After missing the 1st and 2nd strings on the gallops I head towards where some of the jockeys, trainers and local lads meet up before racing to see what's occurring. As in my Friday tips column I am told to fill my boots and have my maximum bet on MINLEY in the opener at Brighton, I took evens, 5/6 and 4/5 for far too much money, after he bolts up by 6 lengths at 4/9 and never a moment's doubt it always seems never enough. Another good winning day.

The other issue that I will be going into later in this book is about the issue of betting every day. As regular readers of my Betfan column will know, Saturday racing isn't really my cup of tea due to the ultra-competitive nature of the day. I do what I do to make a living and a decent profit and don't do it just for show which means that the winners are harder to find on a Saturday even though it's the most popular day for racing.

However, on this particular Saturday I head to Newmarket to watch the racing and find horses to put in my notebook and end up having a drink with a well-known trainer who reveals that one of his best charges will do well in the coming days.

At the end of this day I've not only had a great time but I've also got three horses that I am going to back in the coming week and I will be telling my followers on the day of the race.

The next few days are quite interesting with some bad and good results, including a big bet that gets chinned on the line. The result puts a real damper on the day and I go home to reflect on what should have been a really big win.

The following day, after a sleepless night, I'm really keen to push my maximum bet which is 3/1 early doors. I am quite excited because I have seen it working on the gallops since disappointing at Goodwood and it's been flying.

The jockey is Ryan Moore and despite my run of 'seconditis' the odds shorten and I watch Ryan push the horse into a very good win which means I can relax for the rest of the day and get talking to owners and trainers in the bar to see what I can learn.

With a spring in my step, the following day I put up

three horses and when I arrive at Newmarket I find that my first tip has won well at Nottingham. It's a great start to the day but then:

The picnics are in full swing with the sound of laughter and champagne corks popping until all of a sudden it's drowned out by the most tremendous clap of thunder and the heavens open.

The more posh ones huddle under their gazebos, but it's the others I feel sorry for not knowing whether to keep their prawn sandwiches or their barnets dry, the stiff upper lip, old chap we're English type brave it out under their brollies.

Then the most hardcore have to bolt for the safety of the cars and leave the prawns to swim off, 15 minutes of torrential rain and cowering in our vehicles it's bright sunshine and the only memories are flat barnets and soggy sandwiches and wondering if the stick wielding clerk of course dare still tell his "no non-runners" lie - it's still good to firm.

My only thoughts are firmly with BONANZA CREEK at Newbury now, so we plant ourselves in the owners' and trainers' bar to watch, just as the clerk of the course gives the going as (you got it) "Good to Firm" with Ryan Moore swinging off the bridle 2 out and never a moment's doubt after we win again, backed from 4/1 into 6/4 and we are flying, another 15 points.

Now the pressure is all on waiting until 7.30 at Newmarket for NAUTILIUS at 9/4 for an absolutely fantastic day. There's two hours to kill so I walk to the paddock to have a glance at these mostly unraced 2y olds only to be greeted by the No1 horse trained by James Fanshawe (Hors De Combat) screaming and shouting its head off and more so grandmothers' and children's heads and eyes being rapidly covered, what's happening?? Somebody been injured??

Well, they certainly would be injured if that hit them full in the face!

Hors De Combat has no modesty and no thoughts for us "normal blokes" with his thoughts FIRMLY on the filly in front, racing is the furthest thing from his mind, me and everybody that knows about paddock watching quickly put a line through this sweaty, still very proud playboy and concentrate on the rest.

Just 10 minutes later and 2 lengths to the good (no pun meant) Hors De Combat bolts in, hehehe all the clever paddock watchers have done their money in cold blood and every Granny and sneaky peaking kiddie are drawing their winnings on this impressive "looking" winner.

The day ends with another big winner, it bolts in by 15 lengths, and my loud cheering in the stands attracts attention but it's also an opportunity for me to reflect on how up and down this professional punting can be; on the Tuesday I was so despondent and frustrated and yet three days later everything is good with the world once more.

Obviously I love horseracing and everything to do with it and I support fresh ideas to widen the attraction of the sport to people who otherwise wouldn't be interested. I also enjoy things like the music evenings where a 'big' music act will perform for the crowds when the day of racing is over.

This is what I wrote in my column following the appearance of Meatloaf at Newmarket:

Meatloaf's performance was brilliant last night, but I'm not sure Marvin Lee Aday (Meatloaf) would pass the vet as to my eye he looks a tad lame, although he misses a few notes nowadays, this 65 year old's presence on stage is amazing and the whole group's performance is fantastic; what a voice the blondie girl's got, but sadly Meatloaf your performance was over shadowed by Bellie boys 3 timer heheh, if only...

The following Saturday I had been invited to watch the Norwich and Everton game, because I know one of the big shareholders in the Norwich club and end up having a really great day for what is a 2-2 draw. I put up a few tips for the day's racing and end up with two seconds and a third.

Over the course of the week I have put up 13 bets which led to four winners and seven very unlucky second places. Ultimately though it's a winning week which is what the game is about but it could have been so much better. It's not that I am out of form or relying on poor information, it's simply one of those things that happens.

Ahead of me is the Ebor meeting at York - one of my favourite events and I've already done most of my homework for it. I'm really looking forward to it and know that big profits are coming my way - you need to be optimistic in this game and I will explain more about why this is so and how I use form to uncover really great priced winners.

Chapter Two

York and big profits make me happy

Over the coming days I'm back to having seconds again with some very unlucky losers - two tips lost by a nose on the same day. Despite being very annoyed I have to settle down and work harder on studying form and finding information because I know, like every other poor run of form, this will not last long.

I head to York with my great friend Ian who doesn't know very much about racing (what he does know you could write on the back of a stamp) but he loves the lifestyle so we head to the marvellous city with a fantastic racecourse and get ready to relieve the bookies of their money.

I love York and the Ebor meeting so we arrive the night before and head out. I explained to Ian beforehand that I want a quiet night as this is going to be a long week and I'm here to work. Inevitably, we pitch up at the Living Room, a popular bar by the river, and meet the great Gambling Don - a fellow Betfan tipster. Upon first meeting, I am distinctly unimpressed: he's a bit 'square', something of an anorak but he's dedicated to Betfan, his clients and seems a nice enough bloke.

It's always interesting to meet another tipster and I

wonder what he's really like when I've filled him with some old jungle juice so we can really read the form on him. Even money, I tell Ian, the Don will leave at about 9.30. We head over the bridge to our favourite restaurant which is really busy where the owner Richard employs really good-looking waitresses. We sit quietly eating our fantastic 'rare' steaks - we have them rare because the owner will refuse to cook them otherwise and will ask you to leave if you want them done any other way.

This stance is shortly put to the test when two rather quiet and meek Irish fellows wander in at around 9pm. We all cringe as we hear a shout from the backroom, it's followed by the red wine-fuelled venom that is Richard, who declares that they are late and if they don't like it rare they can leave.

There's just a short pause when one of them, in a very quiet Northern Irish retort, says, "Sorry sir, but we have paid for a room and are staying here."

A rather meek Richard then welcomes them in but then still has the gall to refuse to cook medium steaks for them! Anyway, three bottles of wine later and the Don, surprisingly, is still in the building and is rather more forthcoming than I had expected.

Rather like Frankie was when he was in the house, the Don starts singing like a canary, enough we then head back to the Living Room but we relieve the Don of his anorak as we are crossing the Ouse and throw it into the river.

Rather like the anorak, the planned quiet night has gone out of the window as we re-enter the Living Room again and then end-up staying late into the night.

The following day, the rest of the gang arrives, who I will introduce you all to: Smudger, an ex-City trader, Robert, a currency trader and Dave Horn a vicar, so quite a fair spread of race-lovers.

The first day of the Ebor meeting and its lovely weather and it's very important to kick off the four days on a high and with this in mind I'm up bright and early to get the form done and make all the relevant calls.

I finally settle on three bets: ABOVE STANDARD e/w at 7/1 in the first, ALL THE ACES at a huge price of 20/1 e/w and my main and biggest bet at Lingfield in CAPE FACTOR.

So we all arrive at York Racecourse with all bets placed so we can relax and have a social beer or two and walking through the gates we bump into fellow Betfan tipster Simon Holden who brought me into the Betfan fold.

He looks very professional as he is paddock watching in his Boss suit. We drag him away from his paddock watching, he's not exactly screaming and shouting as we head for the Guinness bar. ABOVE STANDARD is very well backed into being the 4/1 fav as a lot of ours tend to be, but it can't get to the front and finishes sixth - not the greatest of starts.

There's a bit of a wait for the next tip so we get stuck into the Guinness. Five pints later, ALL THE ACES looks fantastic in the paddock and its price is holding firmly at around 20/1. In all honesty he never looked like winning but ran on and got us a place (4/1 winner) so we are now in front for the day with our biggest bet looming at Lingfield. CAPE FACTOR is always handy and the win is never in doubt and he does it cosily at a very nice 7/2. So that's a massive winning day under our belts and I can relax (until tomorrow!).

Now Mr Holden's suit, he has a nice label on the sleeve so we can all see it's a Boss suit and after four bottles of the old pink mixing with the black nectar, we all think it's a good idea, though not Simon surprisingly, that it is removed. We are now hacking at this label with a wine bottle opener until it's off. I wouldn't recommend this practice to anyone and should you ask him he will exaggerate for sure about the size of the hole left in the sleeve.

Now it's time to ply our trade in town, laden with bookmaker's money after making 20ish points in profit for the day, this could be messy as we are already rather tipsy to start with. I grab a quick shower and change into our boy's gear and head for the Living Room once more. The place is Smudger's pet hate but he does comply as does Ian, Robert, Simon and the mad vicar Dave. The older members of the crew are already moaning about wanting to eat, so we head for an Italian restaurant in town. Apart from my lobster masquerading as a Cray fish and Ian's seafood pasta lacking seafood, it's OK. The vicar's nice white shirt looks as if he's been shot with a scatter gun, but I am sure he will get some divine help later to clean it.

The next day it's early to rise after counting yesterday's winnings and not wishing to make yesterday's mistake of not eating early, Ian and I head into town to get some breakfast.

We find a nice looking and obviously quite new breakfast shop and being the only ones in there we order before we notice there are no tables.

Yeah, no tables in a breakfast shop, where does one eat Ian requests and with a 'are you stupid?' expression on his face, the 'chef' replies, outside on the pub next door's tables.

I notice they are also selling breakfasts, rather bizarre, I think. Plastic cups, wooden knives and forks later we leave and I am thinking what happens when the York weather is not so kind? Even money the place is closed before I come back to York.

I get to work and have a huge word for REROUTE who apparently did a sparkling private gallop at home on Saturday, so we took the early 12/1 e/w price and my nap of the day at a huge 9/4 price is THE FUGUE, who in my opinion was only beaten in this race by the rain last year.

I want to back THE FUGUE on course as well, so certainly no alcoholic beverages before the work is done as it's a definite no-no. I never bet while under the influence. I manage to sneak and beg more 9/4 for my hard-earned cash which I am very happy with. In the race, REROUTE is going well on the outside and suddenly falls away leaving me thinking he was on the wrong side of the course, but subsequently I am told he broke a blood vessel, it's a great shame as we really fancied him.

We have an hour until our next race, so a spot of 'sight-seeing' around the crowd is in order, most of the views are stunning, others are 'different' (shall we say) and some are squeezed into outfits that look as if they will explode at any moment, but the overall consensus is, well done ladies - a stunning show.

The most important lady (financially anyway) is now parading in the paddock and looks stunning and my 9/4 is rather like Simon Holden's Boss label, a thing of the past. In the race, our horse gives an absolutely scintillating display and she wins by four lengths in a very quick time. As we show our appreciation by clapping and cheering her in, a job well done, it's another very good winning day. Everything is going well and after racking up another eight points of profit, I'm really enjoying my York trip.

There then follows a quick bottle of bubbles or two and it's all over for another day and it most certainly is for the young lady passed out on the grass.

Into town and we all pass the queue to get into the Living Room (to Smudger's delight) and head for the Slug and Lettuce, with a view to having a Chinese meal later.

As we arrive in town at the Borra Borra bar, I just know my Chinese is now 1.01 a forlorn hope. Robert is drinking as though Black Monday or Armageddon is just round the corner, Ian is quietly gulping vats of red wine, Smudger is doing some kind of audition in Simon's glasses, as he smiles on, oh and me, I am sitting quietly in the corner talking to the Vicar, that's my story and I am firmly sticking to it. We end the night at 2am with classy fish and chips covered in mushy peas.

Up early again to do my work for Friday and I am prepared at 10/1 to take a chance that the drop in trip from 2 miles to 1m 1/2 suits Castilo Del Diablo with Jamie Spencer on board. However, he is hopelessly outpaced and off the bridle early, but does run on strongly but albeit too late though I do note the horse would suit 1m 6f next time out.

My best bet at York is the Johnny Murtagh ridden SIMEON who I think is a good prospect after his good run at Ascot; he finishes a very game second beaten by a head and well clear of the rest and finally we take note of an evening race at Newcastle where we back GRAN CANARIA QUEEN at 9/4. She duly obliges and with the money down she bolts up at a very well backed 5/4 fav. A nice winner at Newcastle and unlucky at York which results in a very small loss on the day.

My time in York comes to an end and, as usual, it's been a hoot and a scoot as I head home for the Saturday meeting at Newmarket. I leave because I'm not a fan of the card on Saturday at the Ebor - but then if it works for all of those hen and stag parties, what do I know?

Overnight there has been a lot of rain and in my column I write:

My selection is very tentative today, coupled with fact that it's a Saturday and the vast amounts of overnight rain. Now that I have surpassed the 100 points in profit mark since joining BETFAN and had a very good winning York, so far, today's bets are going to be kept to the bare minimum. I have decided to swerve the big meetings today as I can see some major upsets and I pin my colours to the HRH horse in the 1st at Windsor tonight, as in my many calls this morning HRH told me she was going to watch from the RH turret at Windsor castle. 11/2 is a fantastic price e/w for MUSICAL COMEDY.

Just minutes after putting the tip up, the price drops to 4/1 and the horse hoses in by 10 lengths. A fantastic end to the week.

I head home, unpack and then repack for my trip to Yarmouth and I'm pleased to note that Louis Steward, the local lad, has ridden another two winners in the week - one of which was a cracker from the front then he rode in the Melrose and snatched a place.

This particular August bank holiday meeting at Yarmouth is a big favourite of mine since I head there with my family which means this annual pilgrimage consists of fathers, brothers, uncles, aunties and wives. We always book into the Palm Court Hotel laden with cases - cases of wine! - and an obscene amount of nibbles which are stored in a room that is picked at random from our booking. Due to my father's room being the poshest and having a windowed turret, we opt for this one and although he has not got to stagger back from anyone else's room after consumption has finished, he has the major problem of sneaking all the empties out undetected the next morning. Not an easy task may I tell you.

Anyway, with all of evidence safely disposed of, I don't know how because father and Pauline rattle past reception like a pair of Spanish castanet players, we leave for the races.

On arrival, I am met by a frantic Quinlan clan man who wants me to represent them and their horse in the first race which I think: "No problem", as I often get the 'odd hint' from them, shall I say.

In the parade ring pre-race I meet the jockey Pat Cosgrave and as they are going down, we all disperse. Five minutes later SWEET ACCLAIM is head-to-head with the Henry Cecil favourite and unbelievably wins cosily by 1/2 a length at 40/1.

Not knowing whether to laugh or cry, as I have only had a scruffy score e/w as you do in these situations, I head back to the ring to meet the jockey, groom and the others before the trophy presentations. There's a screaming commotion at the gate and the wife is let in, clutching a Tote ticket, which of course Tommo (TV commentator Derek Thompson) picks up on like a hawk. After pictures with the horse and jockey we are ushered to the winner's rostrum to receive 'our' trophy, more pictures later and yes, you've guessed it, the microphone is shoved under Sharon's nose.

I cringe at this and with a 'hohoho' from Tommo wanting to know all about this tightly clutched ticket, Sharon reveals that she had £2 e/w at 66/1!

There's a cheer and clap from the crowd, not at all in a sarcastic way, and the mic is thrust my way asking me questions that I have no idea about.

However, luckily for me, when unsaddling I heard the team say: "Wow, first time out and on grass", so with an air of authority I repeat this. Then I am asked about the favourite of Cecil's and all of a sudden I am in my comfort zone again and chatter away as if I'm Tommo himself. Frightened I am stealing the show, I am suddenly and unexpectedly talking to fresh air and Tommo is 'hohoho-ing' again.

As we are heading to the owners' champagne after-race reception, I am accosted by uncle Paul and my father who are glowing and holding the proceeds of their jolly jaunt to the bookies, which I knew nothing about I hasten to add, and both had a jacks e/w (that's a 'jack's alive' or £5) at 50s. Drinking the champers and watching the video of 'our' horse win, I feel like Billy Big B******s, but I'm quietly wishing this all came to light early doors so that all my clients with Betfan would have benefitted as well.

Anyway, that's enough about the Sunday, and the

following day is a huge day not only for me but all of my potential and existing Betfan clients as I have agreed to give 15 selections.

At 5am we leave Yarmouth and by 6am I am already home trawling the Racing Post and thinking I must be barking mad. 8am passes, so does 9am and I've only got three selections. I have pre-warned all of my connections that today is a big day for us all, but all is quiet. Then it's 9.30am and this is when the third lot of Newmarket gallops have just finished when suddenly my phone lights up with contacts calling me, I just manage to get my 15 tips sorted. This is a really stressful situation to be in but there's no-one to blame but me.

My first off is a 5/4 shot from Donald McCain's stable. It leads easily but then tails off at the last. Then the panic starts to begin - what if all 15 lose? Anyway, the day goes well and everyone who was on board should be happy with my efforts - I racked up six winners, three seconds and three thirds. Overall, I finish with a 15 points profit.

I have no plans to go racing this week so concentrate on Epsom but I have two losers. On the Wednesday I head to Newmarket to enjoy the gallops and I am fortunate enough to be with a trainer who tells me the horses names, riders etc without which this is a pointless exercise. There are hundreds of horses running past to make for a fantastic spectacle on a lovely morning, but how do all these professional work watchers really know what is going on?

The short answer is they DON'T, for the main reason they don't know how much weight is in the saddle and without that knowledge they may as well be still tucked up in bed.

After this I head for breakfast and there's always a scrum of work watchers at the breakfast van and it's not a ball that emerges but smiling work riders with breakfasts paid for. They have more idea of how many calories they have consumed courtesy of the 'wanna knows' than the weight they have been carrying in this morning's gallops and anyway most them are still betting in Rupees. I bypass the scrum and head for breakfast in town as that is where the proper news is banded around and I am given a 'proper bet' for Kempton tomorrow night, but nothing for today.

I head home fearing I'm going to have a blank day and suddenly a contact I know as 'Steve the Wrist' calls. He's on fire about two of John Jo's horses running today at Worcester: WHISTLING SENATOR and ANGER MANAGEMENT. WHISTLING SENATOR gets a great ride and wins but ANGER MANAGEMENT seems a tad reluctant to go through with it even with AP's urgings and shirks it, all-in-all a small winning day, but it's a winning day nevertheless.

The next day I am very excited about the information I received during my poached eggs the day previously and quickly scan the Kempton card and yes there she is: RED TULIP.

I am told that she will win but past experience tells me to do it e/w and an added bonus is that it's a better price then we expected at 4-1 and we are going to have a swing at this little filly. Also I have another AP mount in BOLD RAIDER in the afternoon that is very strong so I put this one up as well. I ponder on the double but as one is in the afternoon and the other is in the evening, I decide against it. BOLD RAIDER is pushed home nicely by AP and RED TULIP wins like a dream at Kempton at 9/2. An absolutely blinding day for me and the bookies are stuffed as I rack up a brilliant 25 points profit.

The next morning I'm still on an amazing high after yesterday's winning exploits but I have to refocus on today's card at Sandown. All the dogs from Newmarket are barking 'group horse in a handicap' (the most banded around phrase in racing, and the most ill-placed) which is John Gosden's BREDEN. I decide to go with it and surprise, surprise it's beaten. The excuses immediately start flowing from Newmarket that it ran too wide, slow pace etc but ask Joe Coral or William Hill why they love these over-hyped, under-priced horses. I was very annoyed at following everyone else especially since I know better than to get involved. I issue an apology via my Betfan column to all of my followers.

In my defence, there is a reason for this: I'm trying to turn around what is an unlucky month. My excellent Monday is now a long distant memory and I've racked up 17 seconds. It has still be profitable but it should be better.

It's the last day of the month so I have to make a big impression - unfortunately it's a Saturday and it's an ultra-competitive day of racing. Now I'm faced with a conundrum - do I sit tight on a small profit or do I risk it and try to make a big profit on the day. Obviously, I pile in. This is what I write in my column:

After all the tips and form is complete, I finally settle for two bets. I'm told that BLOCKADE at Chester will defiantly turn over the odds on fav Lilbourne Lass and that Jo Hughes are having a 'go' with CHESTER'SLITTLEGEM at Bath. BLOCKADE slips the field and wins very nicely at 5/2 and we have the perfect start to a Saturday, bit of a wait until CHESTER'SLITTLEGEM.

The so-called super-horse KINGMAN is now 5/1 for next year's Guineas after doing a slow winning time at Sandown, but to the eye looking very impressive, is that 5/1 to get there?

The old warriors Joe and William are already booking their winter holidays on the back of laying the 5s on KINGMAN winning next year's classic. Is it CHESTER'SLITTLEGEM not genuine with a string of seconds now or Cathy? Not wishing to annoy some of you bloggers by being critical of very well paid professionals being tactically inept and being accused of talking out of my pocket I will sit this one out. Grrrrrr. A good winning day but could of been so much better.

Then I add:

Just a quick note before I get slated for last night's comments re Cathy Gannon or lack of them. I saw her in Newmarket this morning and the word on the manor was, in fact, a 'CRAP RIDE' but she has a chance to make amends at Brighton today. We have all had a cracking week to end what was a tricky start to the month with 45ish point profit and with lots in the pipeline.

This is another of the so-called 'joys' of professional punting; no matter how much homework you do, how many beers you buy owners and trainers and no matter how many hours you spend in the freezing cold watching racehorses on the gallops – everything can be undone by a jockey making a mistake. Obviously this hurts when it's your horse that is affected but cheers you up no end when it happens on another horse and yours goes on to win.

Chapter Three

My St Leger 'special' service looms

The flat season is coming to an end and the jumps season is picking up. I gear up for this change over and, incredibly, I agree to do another Betfan special when I provide a day of tips for the St Leger meeting.

Despite the added stress and aggravation, I'm really enjoying my time with Betfan and I'm quite pleased to be asked by Simon Holden to accompany him to help recruit two new tipsters to our ranks. Among them is a very good friend and neighbour in Owen Churchill who used to be a bookmaker but is now a punter and another well-known name from my circle of acquaintances.

Simon drives down to my home and it's the first day of the month so everything goes back to zero and the pressure for profits is back on.

I put up a short priced horse that is trained by Keith Dalgleish and ridden by Paul Mulrennan and though it opens at 7/4 I'm told this is a huge price after its impressive run against the colts at York. However, all does not go well and Mulrennan manages to get beaten.

Now I'm not really a fan of race-goers having a go at trainers and jockeys though a bit of verbal never harms, I am very disappointed to hear the chorus of boos and chants that echo around the Scottish track's ring after the horse's return.

Even more disappointingly, an irate punter actually gets into the ring to have a go at Mulrennan which, for me, is a step too far. I notice too that the Racing Post did well to keep this incident from their headlines.

Unfortunately for Simon, who is travelling down from York, I'm not the best of company after this defeat. I can take losing but I really do hate it when a winner escapes as they are difficult enough to find in the first place. This is an issue I flagged up at the end of the last chapter; despite all the homework a jockey can undo it all.

In the days that follow, Simon and I interview the prospective tipsters and Betfan offers me a chance to run a St Leger special following my previous success which saw me find eight winners on the day and rack up 15 points of profit.

The previous week I had noticed an excellent horse on the gallops called MARTION which I put up as a bet. I also warn Mr Holden that referring to William Haggis as Willie in his Betfan column is not the done thing since he hates being called by that name.

However, we head to a Newmarket pub to watch the racing and enjoy the company of the work riders who are in there. Experience has taught me to be careful who I buy drinks for but Simon has a lot to learn and ends up buying lots of drinks for lots of riders.

I'm pleased to see that my tip does really well, despite looking in trouble two furlongs out but the jockey Ryan Moore does really well and wins at 9/4.

The next morning sees me back on the gallops at 6am and I sidle up to one of the trainers, I dare not mention which one it is, and we both watch an amazing piece of work from a late maturing two-year-old and a classy three-year-old and both are running at Doncaster's St Ledger meeting the following week. Obviously, I will be offering them as tips in my special service.

The day goes really well for me and I have a few winners including a horse I have tissued up at evens and wins at the incredible price of 5/2. At around 9pm that evening I get a very excited call about a horse we 'must back' at Kempton the following night.

This tip means I put out a very early message at 8am the following day to all of my Betfan members offering the tip as a maximum bet. Many of them snap up 2/1 with Corals and Bet365 but the price then disappears into 6/4.

In the days that follow, I prepare to head for a meeting at York and then stop at Huntingdon on the way home and I plan for Tuesday to do my St Ledger homework. This is probably a good time to mention how important the weather is, especially the weather forecasts, for deciding on which horses to back, this is what I wrote after my York visit:

Yesterday's punt was rather scuppered by the mad decision by the clerk of the course at York to water Wednesday evening, I just wonder whether Ladbrokes or Corals are now maybe doing the long term weather forecasting, as soft ground often helps their satchels bulge more, even the infamous Michael Fish could have forecast rain over the weekend, maybe he would have chucked in a hurricane or two for safe measure, but would surely have got the copious amounts of weekend rain correct.

Then I write:

I catch the York to Huntingdon train and arrive in plenty of time armed with a maximum bet at Brighton. OUR CHANNEL runs in the second race and who has been working like a dream in its morning gallops on the heath.

I am just a bit concerned that the rain has followed the Haggis horse box down to Brighton, but am told it shouldn't affect the result but may just temper its turn of foot a shade.

Huntingdon is quite busy for a Monday meeting, although I have nothing to back here today I love the little course and it's a good place to catch up with a few jumps connections for the oncoming season.

An hour to kill and I meet Don Cantalon who thinks his will win the last, Mick Quinlan is quietly confident his will run a big race in the 5th and Tom O Brien thinks Walter White will beat the McCain fav in the 3.40. Dicky Johnson wins the first at long odds on but not without its scares for odds-on backers turning for home. George Baker has OUR CHANNEL well placed 2f out at Brighton and takes it up and for some unknown reason he doesn't take the rail, Hughsey who rides Brighton well at the best of times must think it's his benefit day as he sneaks up the gap left by George Baker on the rail and nabs the race on the line. Hughsey tongue in cheek and with a smirk says in his after-race interview, I quote, "It was very important to get the rail." Well done Hughsey, tactically a brilliant race on not the best horse.

Don Cantalon's bolts up by 27 lengths in the last, Quinlan's runs well without winning and Walter White is backed into favouritism and beats McCain's as predicted, but is firmly put in its place by a 50/1 shocker from the Neil King stable.

One of the best things about being a professional gambler is that winning gives me a chance to indulge in some of my favourite hobbies and take plenty of holidays. This particular week is memorable since I got my 'baby' returned which is a Magenta original Sierra Cosworth with 390bhp - it has spent 12 months in the dock. I bought her after a successful bet in the King George VI on Dancing Brave in 1996 though I could have upgraded my purchase to a Roller if Greville Starkey had not employed such waiting tactics in the Derby when beaten by Shahrastini.

As I could have predicted, with a four day special St Ledger being promoted by Betfan, I am being very unlucky and strangely out of form in the four days prior to the meeting. This is a nail biting time for me and I write this for my column:

I wake early to the pounding of rain on my bedroom window which gives most punters nightmares, but after switching my computer on I see that Oddschecker gives the going at Doncaster as good/firm. The Racing Post gives today's going as good so as always I check with the relevant sites and am rather suspicious about the 'good' going and realising that Oddschecker is generated by bookmakers, I totally ignore that red herring.

Having to select a horse in each race for the next four days, I decide to err on the side of caution and pitch my selections that like the soft side of good going.

All selections are logged and I settle down to watch the racing and I am horrified to see the horses cutting divots out going to the start. Our first selection beats one home and Hughsey reports the ground as soft and especially when the winner's rider Gentleman Ted says the same, oh no I think Bellie Boy we are bang in trouble here. Second race we are beaten in a three-way photo and the third race Medicean Man is not sighted and when Willie Ryan is wishing Benny The Dip was under him and not Winslow Arizona, we are suddenly looking down the barrel of a 15 point loss and only four races gone.

Our main four point win bet in the next and it hates soft going, I am thinking all of the Betfan helicopters are now being dispatched from HQ with primed missiles all aimed at a Magenta Cosworth in Norfolk.

Thankfully the powers-that-be have the foresight to pull out ELKAAYED and Betfan recalls their airborne, for now anyway. The 4.45 and I am not content with one loser in a race, I have two selections in this one; SECRET ART at 9/1 and BRETON ROCK at 14s.

I am watching SECRET ART as it's on the near side and in running is fav on Betfair, when all of a sudden like a flash of white lightning (is it Betfan's missiles I think?) NO! It's BRETON ROCK hitting the front as if it has only just joined the race and bolts in at 12/1 - if you have ever been constipated for seven days imagine the pure elation and relief as you rise from that warm seat, that's me right now, an 11 point deficit and dethroning as the golden boy is NOW an 11 points profit and I have never been so happy as to have another non-runner in the last.

Despite finishing the day with a profit, some members cancel their subscription which leaves me wondering what some punters actually want from such a service. I head to Doncaster where the weather is appalling though I am impressed with those Northern Girls who turn out in great style but end up cowering under brollies to ensure their barnets are kept dry.

Having criticised jockeys for being inept I must also praise them for their bravery and skills too. This is because Hayley Turner has a horror fall from her mount and lies prostrate on the track for some time.

It turns out that she's conscious and moving and there's a slight delay to the racecard. I really do admire jockeys who take a tumble like this and then willingly get back on a horse to do it all over again. Everyone around me had no thoughts about winners and losers as we just wanted Hayley to be OK.

I've had two good days of profits at Doncaster but the third day I spend at home for a variety of reasons. I finish slightly up with one winner, three seconds and a third. For the Saturday's racing I write this:

I have pinned my colours to a horse in the Portland in the shape of STEPS and also EXCESS KNOWLEDGE in the Ledger. STEPS is flying in the Portland and I have hammered it at 10/1 for large sums e/w and all of my clients have had 2pts e/w at 10s. I am screaming at the TV 1/2 a furlong out as I think we have got this only to be done by a nose bang on the line, gutted instead of £1,000s I/we have made a cup of tea. Things go downhill after this and when John Gosden comes on TV and says he has walked the course and in his opinion the "sticky" ground, which we all hate most, will blunt Excess Knowledge's turn of foot.

I think, Mmmmm, wonderful - nothing we can do now and as great trainers often are, Mr Gosden is spot on.

What looked to be a fantastic start in the shape of STEPS backed from 10s into 6s turns in a losing day to finish our Doncaster four day stint. In summary, the weather rather played into the bookmakers' hands or rather the uncertainty of it as the Ledger showed when a 2miler won it, which in itself showed how slow the going had got, but we have another chance next week to beat them as we have the three day Great Yarmouth Festival which I shall be in attendance every day.

I have a couple of very good days and write this:

I am up nice and early, the Post under my arm and heading for 'La Continental Restaurant' for some much needed breakfast. We *have a maximum bet in the 8.15 at Kempton tonight, TRUCANINI which I have already put up to my Betfan clients, so I begrudgingly stop at the Betfred on Regent Road as my two very discreet bettors are struggling to get my full amount on at the early 9/4-5/2 price, which I know will not be there long as it will be smashed up during the course of the day. What a joke these bookmakers really are, they open their doors early solely for the machine playing addicts, but when it comes to a decent bet at a poultry 9/4 they sh*t themselves. Finally after what seems an age of phone calls they offer half my bet at 9/4 and the other half at SP. At least William Hills take the rest without no problem but only at 2s.*

Ham, egg and chips later, courtesy of Richard Senior (La Continental), I feel a bit more human and relaxed after my blood pressure rising bookmaker encounters earlier and set off to the races. I have a wander to down the course and the wind has blown most of the softness from the ground so I now think that it will be ideal for Ribbons in the big race at Yarmouth today and decide to put this up on Betfan but for small amounts as we have had a max bet tonight.

After my bets are placed and to my dismay I find out that Ribbons has had a chipped knee and has not been moving ideally at home, oh crap nothing I can do now so I have to suck it and see. All bets placed and work done, I can relax and enjoy the day's racing and look forward to a very important meeting with a 'top' trainer and see if there is any way we can work together. Ribbons is never really at the races, my meeting is a success and long term it will really benefit me all of my clients.

Coffee in a mug is a great disguise for the brandy and I use this to great effect during the day and it calms the nerves awaiting tonight's maximum bet.

It's good to see Trucanini winning by a clever and very cosy neck and I make another 20 points profit on the day. I take my winnings and along with a few friends we have a really good night out. The next day, I write:

For once I am praying for rain as I stumble for the hotel window to look, Mmmm not yet and our bet today at Yarmouth depends on it. We all have an 8am breakfast date this morning and walking down the cobblestones I can't stop looking skywards and wishing. Breakfast is a very quiet and rather subdued affair this morning and passes without event.

The drizzle starts to my delight and certainly not to all the ladies who are already probably pruning themselves for ladies day at the track. We are pinning our colours to the easy weekend winner OCEAN TEMPEST *trained by John Ryan, who is desperate to get another quick win out of his charge to enhance his chances of getting it in the Cambridgeshire next week.*

With the arrival of the rain I put up OCEAN TEMPEST *at 9/4 and Richard Fahy's in the 1st at Ayr. We don't get off to a good start with a loser at Ayr, so our day depends on John's in the 3.20.*

Ladies in all their regalia are running for any available cover as the rain arrives and I am rubbing my hands with anticipation of another winning day. We look home and hosed a furlong out only to watch our advantage eroded away with every stride, but thankfully we hang on for another winner making this our fourth winning day on the trot.

It's also worth pointing out that while at the racecourse I picked up some very useful information and had tips for horses that day which made me think of offering a service to benefit punters in the minutes before race time.

Over the coming days I enjoy a few good results which cheer me up but still the 'nearly winners' bring me down. This is a tough game and it's no surprise that so few people manage to do it over the long course - I've been going for more than 15 years as a professional and I love it but the stress can be intimidating.

Indeed, I begin a three day losing stretch that prompts calls from Betfan Towers basically telling me to buck my ideas up and I know that after totalling my points for the month so far that I need to improve.

On top of this, clients are starting to cancel their subscriptions which is disappointing since I haven't had a losing month yet and the results are there for everyone to see. It all adds to the pressure to find the winners. I head to the first day of the Cambridgeshire at Newmarket and I write this for my Betfan column readers:

I get a really early text about the young and up and coming David O Meara's Repeater in the 2 miler which backs up my form figures as it ran really well in the Doncaster cup and was unlucky not to be closer to winning, so I rush to take the 7/2 and quickly put it up on Betfan. Just as I am about to leave home for Newmarket my mobile rings and the name displayed really excites me and I am told that the cross ring bit will help Sir Michael Stoute's ASTONISHED immensely in the 3.10 so at 6/1 I also put this up e/w.

Newmarket seems very quiet for the start of such a prestigious meeting but I suppose work is paramount and I am more fortunate than most, which is why I get so annoyed and upset when I hit a losing run because, believe it or not, I DO care and want us all to win. As my readers and clients can probably tell by my writing I am still on a downer but nothing a winner won't cure.

The first race passes without incident but I did pop the Richard Hannon trained Gold Top in my notebook as Hughsey has probably been harder on his daughter for not doing her homework.

ASTONISHED is astonishing as it bolts up by an easy seven lengths and all of a sudden the skies are bluer and the grass is greener but let's not kid ourselves, hopefully this is only the start of a major recovery.

Repeater bombs out and I am so disappointed until Ryan Moore reveals that when the stricken Genzy breaks down in front of him in taking evasive action his saddle has slipped onto nearly its quarters and he can't ride it out fully, I feel a little better but certainly no richer.

The first day of the Cambridgeshire meeting and an 11 point profit so just a little happier.

And this is what I talk about staying the course and hoping that your luck will change. I am so relieved that the draught is over, I write:

I am waiting for the paper shop to open at 6am for my Racing Post when I remember a very good friend of mine, Pete, although he is a Mancunian (but he can't help it) is staying at mine for the last two days of the Cambridgeshire meeting is arriving later. Talk about an avid Man U fan, season ticket holder and, I bet, he can even tell me the circumference round Rooney's ears.

Today, I can't believe that the French raider is 5/1 against the 'good thing' Radiator in the first and as I put up in my column this is a no-brainer bet e/w as you should never be frightened of one horse, so I max bet it e/w accordingly. Keith 'Chatterbox' amazingly gets my full amount on with William Hill which I can't believe but am not complaining about because it saves me various other calls.

William Haggis thinks an awful lot of YUFTEN in the 3.50 drawn stall 13 so I also bet and put this up and finally MORPHEUS in the Silver Cup e/w at 11/2.

I meet Pete at the posh Bedford Lodge Hotel on my way for a quick meet at an Exning Road stable to attempt to find out whether we have got a buzzer to bet for next week.

I would swop the "olop" for a clove of garlic as the French raider passes me heading for the winner's enclosure with the 'good thing' Radiator firmly put in its place (another cruise for Joe and William on all the crazy ante-post 12/1 Guineas tickets) and we have pocketed another 30 points profit oi oi. On my way back to the bar I may even buy a bottle of French wine to celebrate, but I am quite friendly with my liver so I settle for a good 2013 Stella.

I get a bit of a downer on YUFTEN from the powers to be because the course has been widened for the Silver Cup and the stalls are on the far side so now YUFTENS stall 13 is not so appealing because it's out on the flank and bang down the middle. As now expected YUFTEN doesn't win but it's one for the notebook because it didn't get a hard ride whatsoever.

We have backed MORPHEUS e/w in the Silver Cup and it gets us a place and another small win. Very exciting news I get is that our Cambridgeshire bet I have been bulling up all week is 95% certain to go and I will get the call first thing in the morning, I just can't wait.

Another great winning day today with 26 points profit that's 2 out of 2 for the Cambridgeshire meeting and 37 points profit so far. Peter's won just over a grand so he's a happy chappy and even treats me to a posh Italian meal on the way home.

I can sleep well tonight and dream of our max Cambridgeshire bet tomorrow.

Can you guess what happens next? Here's what I write:

8am the call is through and we are maxing EDUCATE in the Cambridgeshire. I quickly put this up to all my loyal clients and advise taking the 15/1 with William Hill for 5 points e/w and I quickly get Chatterbox and Smudger to back it for me at 15/1 and 14/1 for lumpy sums.

11am and I put another two up but all my thoughts and money is firmly with EDUCATE.

We pick up the 'Great Alfonze' and he reminds me and Pete about his milk float story at Cheltenham last year which is an absolute scream, but a story for another day. I tell him he needs to back EDUCATE and to make sure he actually does, we stop in Newmarket and march him into Betfred's and physically watch him put his £100 e/w at 12/1 and then head for the Rowley mile.

Our first loses but without being flippant, I'm not too concerned because the biggy make-or-break tip is getting closer.

*A shout of Andy from the other corner of the owners' and trainers' bar and the trainer Alan Bailey is heading my way with a great big grin on his face, I am rubbing my hands thinking the old shrewdy has a bet for me, but instead he says hold out your hand and he places a tin of brown shoe polish in it and says use the F****r and returns to his crew to rapturous laughter and applause. I had to smile at the old sod.*

EDUCATE looks stunning in the paddock and is definitely the pick, Johnny Murtagh takes him down as quiet as a mouse and for me and us it's whole duck or no dinner time. Johnny settles midfield on the far side group and pounces in the final furlong and makes up EDUCATES mind for him and wins in a photo. We are jumping for joy - we have landed our mini coup and all of my Betfan clients have also had it right off. The Great Alfonze and Pete have both backed it with Roy Christie on the rails at 10/1 to round off a perfect day.

Pink bubbly all round and the party begins in the owners' and trainers' bar, the Great Alfonze's face is getting redder and redder and he looks as if he is about to explode at any moment, Pete for once doesn't seem to care that the Baggies have stuffed Man U at Old Trafford as we drink on and we are the last to leave, having to be ushered out towards the taxis where Alfonze immediately directs him to, yes you've guessed Betfred's. His money certainly never gathers any dust and then on to the Wagon and Horses for a few more sherbets.

Amazing winning day of 80ish points profit to make it three winning days on the trot and amassing an incredible 117 points profit which equates to £1,170 for £10 a point and an incredible £11,700 for £100 a point.

I take the opportunity of urging people to sign up after such a great week of profits and then have a dig at those who left my service earlier in the week. I cannot stress enough that we all have bad runs but we don't panic, we don't change our staking plan and we don't bail out. We simply keep working away knowing that the money the bookies have taken from us on these poor days will soon be ours again.

The following week is the Cesarewitch, one of my most favourite of all meetings and hopefully I can keep this winning form going.

Chapter 4

The unexpected lows after a high

One of the downsides to attending a very popular and excellent racing festival, such as the Cambridgeshire, and racking up a brilliant 117 point tally means that the racing that follows is inevitably underwhelming.

It's a feeling I had in the days afterwards and it's sometimes a struggle to conjure the enthusiasm on low class and ordinary day's racing which, in my opinion, is more difficult to bet and predict than the better class of racing. In addition, it's the first day of a new month which means the pressure is back on to rack up points again, luckily I managed to score 10 points of profit on the first day.

The world of horseracing is in a state of upheaval with news that the televised coverage of Channel 4 is going to be revamped. There are lots of problems with the programme and I state that the coverage cannot get any worse.

It really was a sad day when the BBC announced it was pulling out of horseracing coverage, in the old days both ITV and BBC covered racing on a Saturday afternoon but now we are down to a couple of satellite channels and Saturday afternoon on Channel 4 and a couple of extra days for the big meetings.

The popular jockey, tipster and TV pundit John Francome announces that he's off and will not be working with the new producers which is a massive shame but I won't be sad to see the back of Big Mac after once spending a tortuous train journey to York with him.

The presenting line-up for racing is dated and there are obvious disagreements going on behind the scenes which affects their on-screen judgement.

I compliment a fellow Betfan columnist for his take on the situation and agree that the Saturday morning TV show *Morning Line* could do with freshening-up with better guests. I think the programme should also do better with its tipping for the day and use their insider knowledge to greater effect.

Anyway, over the few days before Ascot I have some decent results and then head for an enjoyable time at Ascot and meet various owners and trainers and have a few beers with fellow columnist Simon Holden.

However, I write this in my column and I cannot stress enough that anyone following horses should follow the going and weather forecasts like their livelihoods depend on it. This is what I write:

We leave Ascot winnerless but as soon as they gave the true going after the first race as soft I realise why our

FOOTSTEPSINTHERAIN never picked up.

It's so wrong and unfair to all of us punters, trainers, owners - actually everybody apart from the bookmakers, that these clerks of the courses keep giving us incorrect going reports as, in my opinion, it's probably the most vital part of the jigsaw.

I head back to the second day of Ascot and with lots of information, which I duly passed onto my members. As I enter the course with Simon Holden and the Gambling Don, I noticed that A P O'Brien has made the journey across from Ireland which is very interesting so I decide to investigate further. Again, we pick up lots of information at the course and use it to our advantage to back more winners.

The day ends with a small profit for my members and I write:

Gambling finished and now we can replace wine gum wrappers with corks and I get a couple of nice bottles of wine (well, the price suggests it is anyway).

Simon is nowhere to be seen and with two bottles of wine, I'm sitting overlooking the paddock; life's a bitch sometimes. All good things come to an end as Simon and the Don both appear and join me at the table, with only one extra glass available, no, no, don't even think it as it can't be done, so I do the gentlemanly thing and go to the bar to get an extra glass.

The TV screens in the owners' bar must still have valves in them they are so old and I am pretty sure it's not snowing at Ascot and I think what a disgrace everything is top dollar in here and we are watching my Dad's first ever TV.

3.35 and the second of the O'Brien's runners JOHANN STRAUSS is settled in last on the outside and JOGS into 4th and leads just past the post, I thought schooling in public was an offence. Watch this is if you can and form your own opinion, but firmly place this Racing Post/Dewhurst entry in your notebooks as we will probably see a different horse/ride next time out.

If it had been a trainer with a rather more chequered or colourful past, shall we say, all the dogs would have been baying for blood or a public flogging at the very least and I wonder if the stewards would have just NOTED the comments as in this case.

I ask Roger on the next table who is watching the screen through his bins (binoculars) how ASCRIPTION the nationwide gamble at Ascot is doing and a short and sharp reply is received: "Crap". So I shut up and think maybe Roger is one of the many Pricewise followers.

Most people who love racing started young and I'm no different - here's my jottings the next day which mention this:

Picking up 79 years young Mr Jolly today and taking him racing at Huntingdon. He loves the game although he has to shoot around in a powered wheel chair now and he comes with me as often as he can. I don't think we have missed a Yarmouth meet this year and I even took him to the Ebor meeting. Mr Jolly played his part in my love for racing and gambling as from the age of 13 I used to hide from the school bus and he used to pick me up and I would accompany him to all the Yarmouth and Newmarket meetings, so now this is a form of a thank you and pay back.

Today's racing at Longchamp is fantastic and I have been many years, but tend not to bother too much now. On one of my early trips when I had what, at the time, was my brains on DAYJUR in the Prix de L'abbaye in 1990 and she bolted up leading all the way by two lengths and as we were staying in Paris that night we went out to celebrate.

The Great Alfonze was part of the crew and we found a nice boozer just across the road from our hotel and with mixed feelings (ok then, at that time anti) about our garlic eating neighbours.

*We settled for a quiet drink, on our own. To our amazement the French chaps couldn't be nice enough and we even started exchanging drinks and even attempting to chat until there was a commotion from down stairs (the toilets) and the VERY red faced Alfonze appeared at the top of them shouting: "Let's get out of here - it's a f*****g queers' pub", and we ran out! We absolutely* *cracked up with laughter and in fairness so did the French, but when a bloody nosed Frenchman appeared at the top of the stairs, we thought we had better move on.*

The end of the flat season is nigh and I am desperate to start work on the upcoming Cesarewitch race over the extended two miles at Newmarket but I am reluctant to do so as we have torrential rain forecast for later in the week and half the field will not act on rain-softened ground.

The following days see me offering tips based on information received and most do quite well but I do tend to get bogged down in doing the homework and studying form for hours on end. It's OK enjoying the races and having a great time but we still have to put the legwork in. All tipsters and professional gamblers have to do this in a bid to outwit the bookies.

Talking of bookies, I actually have a Yankee bet - it's a selection of four horses which offer a combination including win bets and an accumulator. Generally I never do these and I recommend that no-one else does either because they were invented by bookies which means they won't work for serious punters. The best way to make money from a bookie is to place straight win bets for as much as your staking plan is geared towards. Combination and 'special' bets are a distraction that only help the bookie take more money, leave punters with a smaller stake per horse and increase the odds against them actually winning anything.

I admit to getting rather 'stir crazy' being stuck at home and not going to the races. Even a day in a pub and then a bookies doesn't really cheer me up. Also, the predicted heavy rain has come and scuppered my big bet for the Cesarewitch. However, I still have the Irish charge up my sleeve that I was told about at Newmarket.

I head to Newmarket again and find it is relatively quiet compared to other years that I have been though it's probably, as I have mentioned before, due to people having to struggle for extra cash and as with a lot of sports, to actually attend means it's not a cheap thing to do.

The following days throw up some interesting bets but this time of year is a really difficult time on the flat with horses over the 'top' and the ever changing ground conditions, but I have notched up 10 winners so far and lots of seconds.

A lot of tipsters don't enjoy the jumps season but I do since I tend to do very well and I have managed to build-up some of the best contacts around.

I note again how the weather really creates obstacles in finding winners but I manage to find a few and create a small amount of profit. I still get great contacts calling me with tips and I write:

On my way home I get a call and I am told that we have an Anthony Honeyball flyer which runs tomorrow and nothing can get near it at home and they are hoping it will be a decent price, because at home it has been kept well under the radar, so we have something possibly HUGE tomorrow to look forward to.

As I get some decent information from the Evan Williams stable I am excited to receive a very good word on an ex-pointer called MINELLA FRIEND running at Exeter this afternoon and at 7/2 I back this with Corals "in cash" and also advise a 5pt win.

PLEASURE BENT is going really well at home and Hughsy has the ride today and I am told this is going to be smashed up in the betting, so at 7/4 I also back this in Corals "also cash" and take what I am told will be a great price come race time.

A dreary day and it's not made any better by the sloppy jumping of MINELLA FRIEND, which ultimately costs him the race as he is beaten 1/2 a length into 2nd.

Hughsy's mount PLEASURE BENT is being smashed up in the betting all afternoon as I was told it would be and wonder about laying a little of my stake off on Betfair as it's now even money, but that little GREEDY monster is on my shoulder and reminding me of all that CASH that should be coming, so I sit tight "whole duck or no dinner."

No duck or any dinner as a very well backed (odds on)

Hughsy finishes 4th.

What hurts most is I have lost my actual folding, which feels worse than if one of my bettors had put it on for me. Another October losing day. God I'm hating this month!

BIGGY tomorrow, ever the optimist me.

The one thing about a poor run is that the information I receive becomes a crucial element when the weather plays such an important part in what is happening. I tell my Betfan readers:

I wake up excited this morning (now, now only horsey thoughts) thinking about our alleged gamble on a big priced A Honeyball runner and quickly look and try to double guess it as I am not privy to the name yet. I soon realise it's an impossible task and do all my print outs of the form for the day as normal.

Nothing is jumping off the page at me today, so I am waiting for our call, which duly arrives at 10.30am and I am told to spread the money around as much as possible as ROUQUINE SAUVAGE in the 5.40 at Fontwell has been beating everything at home and is in receipt of 7lb.

I am lucky enough to have 4 good bettors and although I have missed the 12/1, I quickly put this up to all my clients on BETFAN and advise a MAXIMUM e/w bet and to take the 10/1. I then inform my crew to take whatever they can for me down as far as 8/1.

Midday this is amazingly 9/4 and I know a lot of you have snapped up the 10s and 8s and the gamble is nearly complete. I hope they have told ROUQUINE SAUVAGE and the final part of the jigsaw is in place when Rachel Green jumps ship as his stablemate is a non-runner.

It has to be the last race and it's an agonising wait as we haven't been particularly pulling up trees this month, so every mishap possible goes through my mind.

All my fears are finally alleviated as ROUQUINE SAUVAGE saunters round the corner about a mile out and wins very cosily. Oi Oi once again the October skies are blue and the grass is green, I have managed to pull off a MAXIMUM bet on a 10/1 winner and we have all had a fantastic winning day.

No big celebrations or lagers tonight, as in the film the Great Escape the tunnel "tom" is now well under way but it's certainly not complete yet.

A MASSIVE winning day of 60 points

As my Maltese counterparts say SAHHA NARAK ADA.

These results really are a 'Great Escape' and help ease the pressure I'm under to continually find winners. Then I get a call saying that a horse called Pendra has been jumping and schooling for fun at home and is the apple of Charlie Longsdon's eye at the moment and could well be the flag bearer for the stable over the fences this year.

From the one extreme to the other: a 10/1 winner yesterday and an odds-on today, but with the very strong information I have received I am not concerned and advise a big bet at 5/6, personally I can only get 4/5 but I'm happy and reinvest some but certainly not all of the previous day's winnings.

Some misguided punters will invest more the shorter the price, but I can assure you it should really be the other way round. Just because a horse is shorter on a bookmaker's tissue it doesn't automatically mean it's more likely to win. I write:

Today I am very happy to back PENDRA at a shade odds on.

The point-to-point boys are crawling all over TRUCKERS STEEL in the NH flat race in the 4.40 at Southwell and the form of its maiden point win couldn't have worked out any better. It's certainly in the right hands as Tom George certainly knows his horses and also his yard gambles. TRUCKERS STEEL is trading at 9/4 on the morning tissues and I take this and also advise the BETFAN clients to follow suit. I have gone in heavier than normal but these boys are good.

We have got some good racing tomorrow at Newbury and Doncaster to look forward to, I am trashed to do the cards yet as this weather is a real pain at the moment and the going could change for the worse.

PENDRAS race is not far off so maybe some dusting or hovering hehehe.

PENDRA does miss a couple of fences but I am never really concerned and he wins for us nicely by 3 lengths, our staking plan today now ensures it's another winning day regardless of TRUCKERS STEEL.

In a nutshell TRUCKERS STEEL is popped out in front and all the other horses and jockeys see during the whole race is his rapidly disappearing hind quarters into the distance and he runs out an easy 10 length winner.

Top information point-to-point boys again, thank you and what an SP, 11/4, BEST ODDS guaranteed comes up trumps again. Another brilliant winning day and another 16ish points in the bin and the tunnel is progressing nicely.

That's two winning days and I'm happy as can be - this really is a game of ups and downs! I head to my local jumps track which opens for business - Fakenham. It's a lovely circular left handed track and the trainers Nicky Henderson and Paul Nicholls love popping short priced runners round here at most meetings.

Fakenham, although on a map it's close to me, the roads are mostly cart tracks and it takes me the best part of two hours to actually get there. It's a lovely morning but we have torrential rain forecast which could be a pain to my punting. I am also honest in my column and the messages I send out to clients. In my column I tell readers:

I am reluctant to put the Gordon Elliot trained ARIANE NOPOLIS up because it's definitely a good going ground horse and if the forecasts are correct, it will scupper his chances and firmly bring the Caroline Bailey charge into contention.

However, it's lovely at the moment and I tell all my Betfan clients if they are able DON'T bet now - wait until racetime as I am.

Second last time and the John Gosden connections think BLESSINGTON can go one better today and are very confident of a win.

My worst fears happen as on my winding journey to Fakenham; the heavens open and we have torrential rain for most of the journey. On arriving at Fakenham the sun is out and I am told the going is good, good to soft in places, I find this very difficult to believe and query the clerk of course's going report in the office, but am told it is correct. Mmmmm.

The first race backs up not only my opinion as it is 30 seconds slower than standard, I ask a jockey what the ground is like and the reply is 'AWFUL'. With my bet pending and with the official going still not changed, I watch the second and again it is 30 seconds slow. I think these going reports are absolute crap and mislead all the racing public.

I decide not to punt, as I said in my column, my worst fears are compounded by him being unable to put his speed to good use and looks as if he has just run the National coming back to the paddock. I have not lost personally, but to say I am pissed off is an understatement.

Henderson and Nicholls both get their habitual short priced winners and we await BLESSINGTON. I also know our fate before the race has been run as the going is now heavy at Newbury and that is as far from what we need as possible. I don't even stay to watch it and listen to the commentary on the way home and we are only mentioned once in the last furlong.

I feel cheated at Fakenham and gutted at Newbury and even worse our good fortunes have come to an abrupt end.

And that readers is racing - all the good and happy feelings disappear as I try to find more winners, only to be scuppered by the weather.

However, come the weekend and my phone rings red hot with information. In the end I had a small winning day which makes me happy since I'm not a fan of Saturday's racing and I'm still in profit for the month - though I've managed 70 points for the week (that's £700 in profit for anyone who follows me at £10 a point!).

Then I set myself a challenge in the column that is sent out to thousands of race fans - I will win 30 points on a Saturday! To help spur me on, and prove I have the connections, I offer two free bets to all of Betfan's readers.

Turns out that only one managed to win but it still helped me make a profit on the day and I get a good reaction from readers which is heartening. What isn't so heartening is the fact that ALL of the racing in the UK is rained off. It's really abysmal these levels of poor weather.

The work, however, for me doesn't stop and I write:

Today we have Great Yarmouth on our racing radars, with a couple of tricky maidens and impossible looking handicaps, in soft/heavy conditions which is far from ideal and with Catterick and Ffos Las both heavy going, it may be struggling today.

Luckily I get a call and I am told that the Mark Johnson stable really fancies DAWN CALLING today at Wolverhampton and after comparing it with my figures and tissue I think the bookies are taking a huge chance pricing this up at 13/2 as this looks a cracking price e/w for a horse with no miles on the clock and seems to have the potential for loads of improvement. I/we snap up the 13/2 with Corals for decent money/points e/w.

It's a typical end of season dreary day at Great Yarmouth with basically only the die-hards in attendance as the holidaymakers have either flown for cover or crept home after their annual pilgrimage.

We see a very nice William Haggis winner (Bilimbi) in the first who still holds a lofty Derby entry, but couldn't have won any easier and an OK Marco Botti winner of the second.

The last race makes sure the greedy ones leave with their exes and more as a 28/1 outsider of the field wins, who previously was a 15 race maiden. I can remember when the last race used to be a get out stakes, but the powers-that-be (bookmakers) have insured more times than not it's an impossible handicap nowadays.

Yarmouth will now batten down the hatches until next April unless the powers that be (ARC) that decide to follow the Folkestone and Hereford route and sell more of the company silver for housing in the close season.

Since it's Yarmouth's last meet of the season I head into town for a few drinks with friends and a director of

Norwich football club. It's a great night: we start at a pub, head to a nice restaurant called Orthello which is run by Michael.

I get the feeling the football club director, who I used to place horses for in years gone by, has more in mind that a 'quiet drink'. And so it proves as we have a few drinks, end up in a lap-dancing club called Bare and then we get told there's a taxi waiting for us all and we are taken the two hours to the Peppermint Rhino club at Heathrow which is a world apart from the club we have just been in.

Then at 6am it's into another taxi and we head to Newmarket to watch our host's horses pound the gallops and then onto Trowse near Norwich to watch the Norwich City players train. By now, I must admit I wasn't in the front of the queue for a jog. Whilst we are watching the players strut their stuff, I get a call telling me we must back Mr Haggis's Crop Report, ridden by Ryan Moore at Newmarket. Me and my big mouth, we are winging our way to Newmarket to do the business but I'm not feeling so great. We punt Crop Report who scoots in by an easy five lengths and, all of a sudden, I can see this going tits up again, so for once my one remaining brain cell kicks in and tells me to get home, which I do.

Chapter Five

It's the jumps season – and I do well

October ends on a high - I rack up 27 points in profit on the last day alone - and I begin rubbing my hands with the prospect at what November will bring - this time last year I made loads of cash. The month starts well and I head to Newmarket and write this:

The owners' and trainers' bar at Newmarket is virtually empty which is handy because I can discuss and sort our big bet in private for next week. MENDIP EXPRESS is first up and bolts home by an easy 12 lengths and we have hit the ground running again today.

Jumping the last I think we have our second winner in the bag as UP TO SOMETHING looks home and hosed until he spots the exit gate and veers towards it and throws the race away and is beaten by a neck into second.

I make my way to the pre-parade ring and our maximum bet NABUCCO looks stunning, although I have got Chatterbox and Smudger to back this for me at 11/10, I decide to walk the rails to fill my boots. The best I can find is Evens with my old sparring partner John Christie (probably the best rails bookmaker left) so I have another monkey (£500) on it.

No room, blocked in and NABUCCO still wins by a neck and we have landed another maximum bet (That's a 90% strike rate on maximum bets!).

In my column I'm also critical of the Breeder's Cup which is a hugely popular contest but I'm not so convinced that it is fair and trainers use all sorts of tricks which are banned in the UK to help their horses win. It also means that the excellent English horses that go there are at an immediate disadvantage. It's a pointless exercise for punters as far as I am concerned and show no interest in it whatsoever.

November begins very well for me and my subscribers as I head to a meeting to enjoy the day and have a very interesting afternoon ahead of me. Apart from the racing I am meeting a trainer with a view to possibly placing his horses. I'm not sure what to expect and I am a bit concerned that this may take up too much of my time, but we will see. The meeting went well and this is a trainer I greatly admire but the proposition isn't for me; although we both end up agreeing that the position needed more time than I could dedicate, however I will be advising on certain races that I think appropriate for certain horses, so me and my followers will be involved if any bets/gambles arise.

The racing world is showing great interest in Exeter

where AP McCoy could be closing in for his 4,000th winner but from a punting point of view, I declare that I will be against his rides for a while as they are all being over-bet and under-priced (and warn readers to beware).

I head to a racecourse for a chat that will 'dot all the i's and cross all the t's' for a promised maximum bet which is set for the following day. In my column I write:

I am pleased to say that our bet is a definite runner tomorrow and it's not just another tipster's old chestnut 'to get everybody to join', then to be told the stable cat has stood on its foot or he has tummy ache and woo behold it's a non-runner (was there ever anything else?) saying this I could still be left with the old preverbal egg on my face if he runs like a ponce after such a long layoff.

100% record today - 3 runs and 3 seconds.

Crazy thing to say you might think, but I am not too perturbed about having a small losing day because once again the information is spot on, although Nicholls pulled rank on Smiley and he had to ride his horse because Daryl Jacob was a non-runner.

Dicky Johnson did exactly what was required and banged UN BON out in front only for him to be beaten by a better horse on the day into a clear second. BREEZOLINI is only beaten an unlucky neck and wins a yard over the line, so two e/w seconds, no harm done and BRETON ROCK is firmly put in his place by a Haggis horse (as we will hopefully see this is a good thing in a weird way).

As long as we continually keep getting on live horses as often as we can, ultimately we will make good profits and that's why, although annoying, we should not be put off or be heading to Beachy Head.

The next day, the nerves get to me and I wonder whether I was quite so wise about being verbal:

I wake up thinking, 'Oh, no! Has the stable cat pissed in our bet's water trough or crapped in his feed and given him the guts ache?' Those and many other weird and not wonderful thoughts because today is a CHUMP OR CHAMP DAY for me after such build-up!

9.20am and I dare not wait any longer as the 5/1 is slowly being gobbled up on EPIC BATTLE in the 3.50 at Lingfield and it must have been an 'epic battle' by everyone concerned after his very bad fall after winning last time out and he has been given over 400 days to recover.

I do temper my enthusiasm a tad and back him MAXIMUM e/w and advise my clients too, just in case all is still not right in his mind after such a horrific fall.

Although our day will evolve firmly around EPIC BATTLE

I do put up two more: BOUCLIER which I am told is eating up the Newmarket gallops for Luca and BRAVO RIQUET who loves Towcester and is very well in himself.

I am getting loads of texts from my avid Betfan followers saying thanks for the FREE tip, what free tip I'm thinking; I've not given one since advising 'not to eat yellow snow' on Sunday (which prompted one person to email asking what time does it run heheheh!).

The penny drops as Betfan Towers have cottoned on to our 'good thing' and nicked it as their freebie and emailed it out to half of the population; God I hope all my members have got on OK.

I am now going to have the old barnet trimmed and then onto The Chequers to watch the racing with the lads and settle the old nerves with a sherbet or two.

Sat watching the race I see that Epic Battle is rearing in the stalls and comes out stone last, a groan and a deadly hush descends on the pub and all eyes are on the plonker with the big mouth huddled in the corner.

Liam Jones is kidding him along and a slap or two down the neck doesn't fill my baying audience with enthusiasm, until miraculously as the camera angle changes, Liam has dived for the rail and he is flying. The nervous, quiet huddle, me, has emerged from the corner and is now roaring like a tiger all the way to the line and Liam and Epic Battle have done it by half a length.

The Big Mouth (me) is glared at and told off from behind the bar for the noise pollution, but who gives a flying f##k! I've just earned his year's wages, maybe in hindsight, if he had been part of the gamble, maybe a bit of slack would have been cut.

I go onto enjoy my winnings in the only way I know how and then I write:

Not EVEN a mention from Betfan Towers that 'I' have given half the country a 5/1 winner, maybe a gold watch is winging its way to me or if this has pissed them off, maybe two tickets to listen to Simon Holden's webcam.

Even worse not even one person signs up resulting from the winner; good job I punt all these as well and do this for the love of it (is anybody out there?) and we are also second in the Betfan table - what do we need to do?

Maybe 'The Tower boys' have a masterplan up their sleeves for us established ones as well as the new?

What do you all think? Even money this bit hits the cutting room floor Sunday morning heheheh.

It didn't end up on the cutting room floor! And no-one replied about my thoughts. I'm really enjoying my punting and letting my followers know about the information and contacts I have that throw-up great winners at 5/1 after a 400 day lay-off. It's a crazy world and if that sort of service doesn't impress then, I guess, nothing will.

Another query racegoers often ask is apart from getting information, how do I use the stats that abound nowadays? Perhaps I'm one of the old school but I don't think you can actually beat having the paper, especially the Racing Post, although it is impossible to work without being online nowadays as the information is instant and bang up to date. Then you just need some peace and quiet to go through the form and news from the trainers and owners as well as taking on board what other tipsters are saying. The ultimate decision though is usually mine about which horse I will back.

In the days that follow I head to Doncaster which is a great racecourse and I write:

Doncaster has its normal cat walk show ready for us, all of you that have never witnessed it surely must. If I ever dare risk a stay over in Doncaster, I am going to trot into the town centre and check whether it's the girls or the shop's fault that nothing over the size of 12 is ever worn regardless of the physic being crammed into it.

Although the sun is shining, I have witnessed ball-less brass monkeys and still the pretty frocks are, Mmmmm, very summery and the girls are most determined to show off their ample wares in these less than ideal conditions.

If I had a hat and it wasn't too cold to take it off, I surely would to these flaunting diehard beauties!

RHOMBUS is now trading at a crazy 6/1 and now I am armed with my Racing Post I can see why I have clashed with Pricewise. Although he is the most followed tipster in the country he is bang in a vein of poor form, so I am not ecstatic about this.

Mr Haggis is chasing the 100 winner landmark and unfortunately blows out the first of his runners with one more remaining. We get off to a great start when Smiley puts in a brilliant ride on WONDERFUL CHARM after awful mistakes at the last two fences and gets up right on the line.

Our fate is sealed early as SDS is shuffled to the back after a tardy start on RHOMBUS and we are being shoved along all the way, although SDS never gave up to his credit we were never going to feature and yes the cream always rises to the top and Mr Haggis bolts up with CONDUCT and not only wins the November handicap but seals his 100 winners with his very last runner of the year.

We are now lucky enough to be in profit for the day regardless of what happens to HELLO GEORGE in the last. Another great ride gets HELLO GEORGE up after looking beaten for most of the way and Dicky Johnson seals a very good winning day for us. Two really good, strong rides has resulted in a 9ish point profit for us today and both should be up for ride of the week, somehow I think winner No 4,000 will get it and rightly so, well done AP.

The week continues well and I write in my weekly column:

Another great day's punting yesterday with once again our FREE advice MINELLA FORU winning and turning over the short priced fav. That's two freebies I have given this week and two winners - must soon be time for 'Arise Bellie Boy'.

Oh, and hats off to 'The Tower Boys' for leaving the Sunday morning cutting room floor clean.

Seriously now, we have an exciting and very busy week ahead of us. Starting with Huntingdon on Tues (then on to the Oakham Weatherspoon's opening) and the great Paddy Power meeting at Cheltenham Fri, Sat and Sunday, which for me is unmissable, not forgetting our MAXIMUM bet squeezed in between for good measure.

Today looks relatively quiet on the tissues, although we have three meetings. One of great interests is TUTCHEC, who was one of many to help AP in his unprecedented quest, stands out, I have this tissued up at 5/2ish and it's trading at 7/2. I know he is up in the weights and in a stronger race but the information that he has had three weeks of intensive jumping at home and should negate these two factors.

In the end, I decide to get Chatterbox to back this horse at 7/2 for me and also put him up as a win only bet to my clients. Also, as only my clients are privy to, I pop a "liddle luv note" at the bottom of my email advising them to back a certain 12/1er e/w.

I am wanting to update my winter racing attire and as I always say, we must spend some of our winnings and then it's much more appreciated and tends to add more value to what we have achieved and we have been winning loads in recent days and weeks. So I head to Newmarket and Goldings on the High Street to get a new coat, scarf and boots and with a few extras and a monkey (£500) is soon winging its way to the till.

When your luck is in, everything just seems to drop into place and as I am walking back to the car, I bump into an old betting contact and owner that has had a year out of the game; he really was top drawer and we used to work really well together.

We pop into a wine bar for a catch-up and a sandwich during which, I explain what I am doing with Betfan and my own tipping line and luckily he is well back into it and has horses scattered around with certain trainers. I then tell him we have backed one in the next and that I need to go next door to watch TUTCHEC run. I have another cash bet at 4s e/w and so does he.

Thankfully, TUTCHEC leads all the way and wins really well. Good old 'Fred' (Betfred) has just paid for all my clobber from

Goldings and all of a sudden the boys are back in town and a year, all of a sudden, seems only like yesterday.

Over the next bottle of wine as a way of thanks for today, he explains to me that he has been told to heavily back a horse at Wolverhampton tomorrow night and although it's going to be short it WILL win. On departing I mention our 12/1er tonight and head home. It's been a great winning day for me and my service; not only have I backed a 4/1 winner I've also managed to rekindle a relationship with one of my shrewdest gambling pals around. To further cap a super day, our late night 'nameless' charge gets us a fast finishing place and with a better draw would have won.

Two weeks into November and I'm sitting on a 60+ points profit (or £600+ to my followers) and my strike rate for winners is running at 50% - that's pretty impressive and I'm very pleased with my work.

I give my old friend the name 'Fred' after our enjoyment in the Betfred shop and I tell all of my members the following day of his tip at Wolverhampton. I send out an early email and the price is already at evens - I tell everyone to climb on board because this one will be odds-on when the race starts. Later, I write in my column:

I am gracing Huntingdon with my presence today and will

be leaving relatively early as it's a 12.40 start.

Before I leave I also email ITOLDYOU as a small e/w bet at 8/1 and a stronger e/w on ELSPETHS BOY tonight at 11/2.

Huntingdon is busy today as it has two receptacle days for annual badge holders from Cheltenham and Sunny Yarmouth.

I'm not planning to have a bet here today because I already have a small fortune laid out, but you never know what you might hear or learn whilst actually on track.

The first race passes with what now almost seems the norm with AP adding to his possibly already insurmountable total.

However, whilst having a cuppa in the owners' and trainers' bar, I do learn that the reason Alan King and his owner Simon Bullimore are in attendance is to watch their SUBURBON BAY run in the second as they think it has been crying out for soft ground and today is the first time he has encountered it and they are hoping that it can win. I don't go mad but have a nice bet to cover the day's exes at 10/3.

SUBURBON Bay is always bang there and bolts up by 30ish lengths with its head in its chest, right place at the right time (when things are going well). A small knock as our first bet at 8/1 is always up with the leaders, but just misses out on a place and comes home 4th

I leave before the last NH flat race as I want to be home in time to watch INTERCEPTION run in the 4.50.

Gentleman Ted is a bit further back then I would have liked at halfway on INTERCEPTION but as soon as he brings him to the outside it's goodnight nurse and he absolutely bolts up by 3-4 lengths at odds-on and we have landed another MAXIMUM bet at Evens (over 90% strike rate on Max's now, I think??) and we are cruising to another winning day with one to run.

ELSPETHS BOY tries his heart out and at one point (as do the in-running punters as it's a shade odds-on) I think we are going to cop again, but ultimately he just comes up short and nicks us a place and a small win to cap another FANTASTIC winning day.

Despite the great day I know that I have to refocus again and keep my feet on the ground. I write:

After yesterday's great day I should be heading up to the city this afternoon to complete my winter shopping, but instead I am going to start doing the Cheltenham, Paddy Power card as I think we could have a big price sleeper on Saturday and I want to check it out against my figures.

Also I have just been informed that I am in week 12 of a tipster checking system done by a company called BETTING SYSTEM TRUTHS and my allotted man is a Sgt Brian, personally I have never heard of them and don't know how long it lasts, but it should make interesting reading when I find out more hehehe hope it's all good. I will keep you all informed when I know more.

In recognition of my successful free bets, Betfan really does give me a big push which I really appreciate. However, I set off at 5am (I told you, it's not all glamour!) for Cheltenham as it's nearly a five hour drive, depending on traffic. The Cheltenham journey goes really well and I arrive at 10ish and the flat I have hired is very satisfactory and although I state I must have Wi-Fi, I have an added bonus because it's a really quick connection, but no French maid in sight which is bit of a blow.

I am surprised by the amount of people that are here on the first day, so I creep into the Press Room to get out of the way of the hustle and bustle for a while. There are no winners in the few tips I put up so I head for the Betdaq tent for free food and alcohol. I write:

Far too much Betdaq wine and I am already racing and with a long night to come, will I ever learn? Back into Montpelier and Ladbrokes to watch, what turns out to be a disappointing second from BEAUTYS, so not a good day and our first losing day for what seems like forever.

Cheltenham is really buzzing and we are not planning on a crazy one, so we book into the Chinese called Ruby's, which I think is one of the best in the UK.

We just pop into the wine bar for a night cap and things go tits up from then on. We visit the Piano bar where a pianist plays all night and he is amazing. All the Betdaq and Chronicle bookmaker boys are in there and the drink is flowing and the atmosphere is brilliant. Think it is 2am when we finally leave.

For the next day's racing I've already tipped a couple of high price outsiders for e/w fun and I write:

Outside of the Cheltenham Festival, this is one of my favourite day's racing of the jumps year. Cheltenham is packed and really buzzing, we start off with the habitual hot toddy and wander to the parade ring to have a look at our first bet ROYAL IRISH HUSSAR. He looks amazing and you can see why the Ballydoyle boys advised Nicky Henderson to send their ex charge here for this race.

ROYAL IRISH HUSSAR never looks like anything other than winning and does it really nicely and he must be one of the favourites now for the Triumph hurdle. A great winning start to the day. Our 33/1 shot ATTAGLANCE is getting smashed up in the betting, as I said it would, and goes off at 16/1.

We are always up with the lead, but a few sloppy jumps and we drop back and I think we are doomed, but somehow he shows real guts and determination and runs on really strongly and nicks us a place and lands another super punt for us.

DANCING ART never really gets serious until 2 out and I

think the lack of race fitness told and we are unplaced.

We have had another super winning day of just over 16 points. We jump on the races bus and head straight into town with more than a spring in our step. We must still be top of the Betfan tree with something approaching 85 points profit for the month.

Turns out that despite my best efforts - and I did avoid the perils of the Piano bar and Bar 21 - it was another late night and a great time was had by all at Cheltenham.

The following week I head to Fakenham and promote a horse that starts at 12/1 but which will be heavily backed down. Simon Holden comes along and we enjoy a drink with some of my friends. In the end my big tip opens at 4/1 so our 12/1 looks like amazing value and the drift doesn't concern me too much as I know all the live money is already on.

I know the instructions are to hold him up and slowly ease into the race but I must admit I wasn't confident of victory at halfway but as soon as he is asked, he absolutely flies and wins with consummate ease. This is a great win and means I have now surpassed 100 points in profit this month.

Chapter Six

I'm an honest tipster

I really am flying when it comes to the tipping and I'm so pleased and proud to be more than 100 points up. I'm also excited about the prospect of two huge days of racing at Ascot and then I have Haydock to look forward to.

I actually drive myself down to Ascot as I want to leave before the last race as the M25 is an absolute nightmare on a Friday evening. Turns out it was a losing day and it was a long drive home though I did note a few great horses with potential. Again, I'm really down and the long trip means I have to contemplate the dip in form after such a great run.

The next day I get to work early and I have a friend giving me a lift but I'm not ready when he arrives so I have to cry off. It's a long trip by yourself so we agree to go to Huntingdon instead which is only an hour away. I'm deluged with information and spend a long time going through it all.

My first two tips perform badly and then the third lets me down too but my fourth manages a win. It's a loss on the day and I'm disappointed to note that I'm no longer on a profit of 100+ points but now down to 85 points. That's still a great result for tipping but I know it should be more.

Anyway, my confidence isn't boosted by a free tip I

gave all of the Betfan readers. Here's what I wrote afterwards:

Yesterday's free tip was absolute crap and a total embarrassment and was never at the races, which was very disappointing because the info I had received was very strong, although all of my members had a good winning day thanks to the last race at Naas and a fantastic SP of 3/1 on SHESAFOXYLADY.

So very nice to finish another week on a high and a winning note (88pts profit for the month so far). My goal which starts today, is to smash the 100 points profit barrier again for this month and build on it.

Those are bold words and I intend to work harder to get there. Over the coming days I knock the winners in and the points start to build again and then at the end of the month it's Hennessey Day - a great day in the racing calendar. I write this:

Hennessey Day and what a fantastic race it's going to be as well, 10/1 the field - one of the most open I can ever remember. I am not going to be present this year, which is a shame because it's a race and a day I do enjoy immensely.

With such an early start I find I can't get all my work done in time as it would mean leaving home at around 9am.

I am told that Alan King has got INVICTIS as fit as he can at home and it's very well fancied to go very well after such a long lay-off. It's trading at 10/1, paying the first five places so we need to take the 10s and back it e/w.

Steve is once again all over MENDIP EXPRESS and his mate William Biddick is doing the steering again, after his very cocky win on it last time when we backed it. 5/2 is a very fair price, I think the price is holding up because the McCain's are trying to win the race that is named after the great man Ginger himself.

Our day is completed with THE DRUIDS NEPHEW which at 10/1 with the Tote I think is a cracking e/w bet.

MENDIP EXPRESS is still weak in the betting and drifting. Obviously nobody told Biddick and MENDIP because he is always travelling very well within himself and wins very nicely at an amazingly good price of 3/1. Great start to the day with two more to run.

Just when you think all is going really well THE DRUIDS NEPHEW falls at the first; the ups and downs of racing.

INVICTIS cruises up on the outside and trades at a very short price in running, but ultimately runs out of puff after his very long layoff, it is only money lent because he will win next time out.

A nice winning day to finish off what has been a fantastic winning month, we haven't quite hit our goal of finishing over 100 points profit for the month but we are in the high 80s and will be very close to the top of the leader table for the month.

Then I move on to the Christmas run-in. This means that every tipster and punter will be overusing the phrase 'this horse is our Christmas money', so beware as it only actually comes off a very few times. I got my Policing Review of systems completed, which finally gave me a pass with 4 stars out of 5, after a fashion. I was unfortunate enough to have a new recruit, who obviously knows very little about both betting and betting systems (Sgt Brian) and whoever gets him next I wish them all the very best. He seems to think ROI is not an important part of betting and has the power to downgrade a part of the Betfan system with 4 out of 5 stars (support) which he says he never used.

I personally was very pleased with 112 points profit over the 84 day review, but for some reason he wasn't.

Thanks to James, a more experienced member, who obviously knows his onions, had to oversee the poor failed gambler Sgt Brian and correct him in the error of his ways.

Sgt Brian will probably continue reviewing systems, badly for now anyway, as it's a nice way for him to keep getting FREE tips in his retirement.

But, hey ho, I got a 4 star pass, which is very good as they say most fail and 99% are tanked up and overrated, let alone get a star rating. This is what I wrote:

DRAW YOUR OWN CONCLUSIONS (below I have copied and pasted from their updated review, by James).

Subscription Cost: 90 Days Great Deal at £130 for the quarter.

WIN BETS 124: Payouts 46 = approx 37%

E/W bets 105: Payouts 41 = approx 39%

10pt(win/ew) 25: Payouts 11 = approx 44%

Average strike rate of 40%.

PROFITABILITY

Working from a bank, I feel the increase of the bank is more important than ROI however a 42% ROI in 3 months is excellent.

Betfan tipping services never recommend anything beyond points per selection. We can look at some results based on the following stakes per point.

£2 Stakes = £225.04 – Gross profit on the tips sent. After the cost of subscription (-£130) you would have netted +£95.04

£5 Stakes = £562.60 - Gross profit on the tips sent. After the cost of subscription (-£130) you would have netted +£432.60

– – – – – – – – – – – – – –

In the welcome email for Andy Bell Racing it is advised to use a £2500 start bank with £10 stakes (=250 points)

£10 Stakes = +£1,125.20 - Gross profit on the tips sent. After the cost of subscription (-£130) you would have netted

+£995.20

– – – – – – – – – – – – – –

£20 Stakes = £2,250.40 - Gross profit on the tips sent. After the cost of subscription you would have netted +£2120.40

£30 Stakes = £3,375.20 - Gross profit on the tips sent. After the cost of subscription you would have netted +£3245.20

£10 stakes is not an unreasonable stake advised which is realistic and a nice profit of £995.20 is achieved after you have paid for the service. Returning a 42% ROI is also not to shabby and much better than 99% of the tanked up overrated products on the market at the moment.

Rating 4 Stars Out Of 5

EASE OF USE

Nothing could be simpler email in, bet out, 14 bookmakers were mentioned.

Rating 4 Stars Out Of 5

RISK FACTOR

Andy Bell racing averaged a cool 40% Strike Rate which is pretty much up there and worked perfectly with his money management advice.

Rating 4 Stars Out Of 5

Overall Rating 4 Stars Out Of 5

ANDY BELL RACING has his own records going back to may, which to me are accurate, you can find them at the link below.

Thank you for your time and I hope you have enjoyed the review.

I'm open and honest enough to report this to the Betfan readers and ask anyone with an opinion or a review of my service to get in touch. All-in-all the figures are very good and an overall hit rate of 40% is very good - though I know I can do better.

On the racing front, I had no plans to attend any meetings for a while but was gearing up for Huntingdon and Cheltenham again. After a few days of visiting friends and contacts in London and then deciding against going to Leicester, I spend the afternoon in a good pub to watch the racing. Then I write this:

I sent out an e-mail last night urging all my members to hoover up the 11.10 on ROLLING ACES at Sandown today as I knew this was going to be well punted and go off at odds-on.

Fridays are normally a real busy day at this time of year as I like to start looking at the Saturday cards, because everybody loves a Saturday winner, but the trouble is ALL the trainers and owners do as well, so they get some decent coverage on TV and the trainers are then more in the public eye and have a better chance of attracting or enticing new owners to the yard. This makes, in my opinion, Saturday the hardest day to get winners and if you take a minute to analyse the results maybe it will come apparent how difficult it really is for us humble tipsters as well.

The reason I start Saturday's cards on a Friday is because of the early starts and if I go racing I have to leave home around 10ish and there is nothing worse than leaving in a rush and half-cocked, because if your head isn't right in this game, mostly you are doomed to failure.

Just as we were today, doomed to failure ROLLING ACES was in fact very well punted into 8/13 on, unfortunately, I didn't factor in that VINO GREGIO was going to put in his first near faultless round of jumping of the year and win like a good thing.

The Moore father-and-son combination just wanted him to get in a clear round of jumping to boost his confidence and they never expected him to actually win. But hey that's racing, once again (although to our detriment today) we are reminded that these 1 tonne beasts of beauty are not machines.

Well, anyway apart from all that bollocks we ended up having a losing day.

One of the big issues I have is that I have problems going into betting shops. I will probably deal with this later in the book but essentially the staff are told to look out for me. Bookies today don't really ban punters any more for winning too much money (though I am barred from several shops) so instead they make it difficult to put a bet on in the first place. They will query the money and offer lower odds if they suspect they are dealing with Andy Bell. This means I have to use trusted aides to go put bets on for me but I have another issue and I write:

Today, I have the unenviable task of placing some of my own bets, as I have a stewards' inquiry with one of my putter on-ers, which pisses me off immensely, as we were all on to a good thing. May be it's my easy going nature or may be some people just can't help themselves and are just greedy bastards.

After what I am sure will be a fashion, as in all the Ladbrokes shops I am known as a 'Shane Warne-lookalike' and not overly welcome, I hasten to add. Unfortunately it's not because I am shagging the gorgeous Liz Hurley, I shall need a beer or three and my column will probably be illegible, so until tomorrow, Caw.

I'm not joking either! This how Ladbrokes staff recognise me! Then I write:

It wasn't as horrendous getting on yesterday as I thought, but I will say these multi-million pound companies don't like or are not allowed to take a bet with a liability of more than £1k without being checked, so if you keep your winnings under that magic figure, it's possible to keep under the radar, for how long I'm not sure.

Let's just hope the queues of 'goat feeders' (roulette machines, we call them 'the goats' because they just gobble up everything that's put near them) keep the greedy ones opening at 7am and 8am, because us humble punters could never achieve them keeping such early and late hours.

Seriously, why does anyone bother with those machines? There are blokes who spend their entire day sat in front of them.

I can't think of anything worse though I did encounter one couple in a betting shop who must have had a huge win because they were so skittish when I approached the counter to get a bet on. It's not like they were handed bundles of cash - the staff member put the money on their bank card and then they returned back to the machine to start spending again! Quit when you are ahead people!

Anyway, enough of my moaning - December really sprang into action when two winning tips won to bring a 40 points profit for the day. This is just the fillip I need and I tell readers that these times lead to the winners simply leaping of the pages of the Racing Post.

I'm still following the career of a young jockey and I write in my column:

The Yarmouth contingent are backing their up-and-coming star this morning Louis Steward who rides the William Stone trained CLOCK OPERA. Louis rode an exceptional race on this last time after being rather bullied to the back of the field at the unusual flip start by his more experienced counterparts and then having the last laugh by nutting them all on the line and winning.

Today from his inside draw, I assume he will be bang up with the pace and nick it with his good turn of foot. Trading at 5/1 this is surely a bet to nothing e/w as I can't see him out of the three and looks one of the more very likely winners.

Last week's diary was bit of a battle of wits between me and the Tower Boys, as I had hinted, I was going to write some rather unfavourable things about my review and reviewer.

My cunning plan was to send it through as late as possible to put them under pressure (10am it's required) and hopefully it would then just get pushed through the system unedited, which I did at 10.45, but ultimately the cutting room floor won and it must have taken most of Monday to sweep it all up.

The reviewer is allowed his views and allowed to affect my business, so as long as mine are constructive and no swearing, why am I not?

Anyway, I'm still reluctant to offer my views though most people can guess what my thoughts are about the 'review'. I've also managed to recruit a new putter on-er in the shape of Chippy Pete so I'm pleased about that. I'm even more pleased that my bets rack up 70 points in profit in just three days though Louis let me down by getting beaten by a nose in his race. This is what I write:

We awake this morning to see that we are once again way out in front at the top of the Betfan tree, closely followed by my old mate the banned bookie Betowen, which just shows how well things are going from our neck of the woods. I hope Sgt Brian isn't still getting my tips for FREE.

Today, as I said in my daily email, that MUTHARIS is schooling and jumping brilliantly at home and is expected to be backed into favouritism and win today on his debut. At 15/8 I get on and advise all my merry followers to do so as well. Nothing else worthy of our hard earned today.

Not a great start as the 12.07 train is cancelled and we have to wait for the next in 30 minutes. I listen to MUTHARIS on my mobile and although he seems to fluff the first two fences after that it sounds as if Denis O'Regan is very confident of his mount's ability and wins quite nicely. So another winner and I expect we increase our lead at the top of the table.

Once again this month we are hitting an amazing 52% ROI and just over 33% of winners and are already nearing the 50 points profit for the month.

So another really nice winning day, that's four real good winning days on the trot.

I'm not at the race as I'm heading to London and meet Smudger at Liverpool Street and we go for a coffee just to sort our strategy for our coming meeting.

We meet our contact opposite the Bank of England and head towards Harry's Bar, rather posh and priced to suit, I hasten to add that I'm relieved that I'm spending the bookies' money.

With the meeting complete with just a few I's to dot a T's to cross, we hit the town. Unfortunately, I miss my 6pm train home and I eventually stagger onto the 8.30 and before we are out of the tunnel I am gracefully snoring and probably annoying everyone within earshot.

And no, it didn't happen; I didn't oversleep my stop. That's only because my lift home was constantly ringing my mobile and though it's not awaking me from my slumber it has, apparently, awoken everyone else. This is put to rights by a sharp dig in the ribs by my now totally pissed off neighbour and he alerts me to the fact. It's my lift awaiting at the station inquiring as to my whereabouts though I have to confess that I'm nowhere close to being home which means I'm in trouble again. This is what I write in my column:

It's all rush, rush this morning as we are leaving at 10ish for Huntingdon as it's a 12.30 start. It's Huntingdon's biggest day of the year as it's the annual running of the Peterborough Chase, which looks impossible as a betting proposition, but should be a good race.

Happy days the Quinny lot are on the blower with another 'good thing' of theirs running at Newcastle today in the 12.20 RACING PULSE a shade odds on, but for once I am not overly concerned because we have had 4 out of 4 so far this year. I pop this on my email and also have a real swing at this at 5/6 via my merry band of putter on-ers and I even invest real cash early doors at Corals.

The troops have all rallied around and we are bombing up the A14 because all of a sudden the 12.20 at Newcastle has just become more important than the Peterborough Chase. We arrive at 12.10, Mr Jolly's whizzed up trolley is literally thrown together and we head into the owner's and trainer's to watch our so-called flyer. The money is well and truly down as it's been smashed into 4-6, so

5/6 doesn't look so bad now, coming round the top bend I wish I could get some more 5/6 or even 4-6 or even 1-5 as it's absolutely pulling the old proverbial fish cart and wins with its head firmly in its chest by 17 totally untroubled lengths.

Cabbage Paul has smashed it in the on-course Betfred and got his days exes and more, Biggles Steve has cleaned-up from wherever he cleans up from, Chippy Pete has smashed his mobile to pieces as he called just as they were jumping the first and we have all had another amazing winner and racked up more points and more importantly eased some more folding out of the greedy ones.

Tinned Guinness isn't so bad after the first four or five, honest, it tastes OK. Ish. Hats off to Barry Geraghty for never giving up in the Peterborough Chase aboard Riverside Theatre as he was out with the washing coming round the top bend and he pushed and shoved and never gave up and got up bang on the line, surely must be up for ride of the week.

Another brilliant day and that's an amazing six winning days on the trot.

In the middle of December I am topping the Betfan Tipster's table - how about that Sgt Brian?

Chapter 7

Tipping doesn't get any easier

In addition to writing regularly to my subscribers, I also write a fairly popular column for the Betfan newsletter which gives me a bigger platform to offer my opinions and expertise. As part of this, I also get to offer a free bet for readers.

However, if the free bet wins at a good price, it means that my regular subscribers can feel aggrieved at having to share the information that they have to pay for. In my defence, it's a good way to advertise my skills at bringing profits to people who enjoy horseracing.

So while finding regular winners is very hard work and often stressful, the job of finding an impressive free bet on a Sunday is very difficult indeed. As I've said before, Saturday punting is notorious for being difficult but I try my best but Sunday racing really is a different world.

Halfway through December and in addition to the weather adding to the problems of winner selection, I've had a poor run of non-runners too. In the week after I provided a 9/1 winner as the free bet, I then had five non-runners.

Despite this, I'm also topping the Betfan tipsters table for the month and one day head to Fakenham where, for a change, it's not the coldest course in the country. I've taken my friend Mr Jolly for the day's racing and for the excruciating journey to the course.

Two horses from the day's card are put up and the first one never really travels and gets easily beaten which makes me despondent and then I put a bet on Carobello and go stand by the first fence to watch the race. This is what I wrote in my column:

I am not always the most compassionate person when a horse falls, but when CAROBELLO stops right in front of me near the first fence, I am shocked to see the poor thing has a stick that has gone right through its muscle and is sticking out of either side like an arrow. Which makes my £600 loss on him suddenly seem a little insignificant.

Not a good day at the office and we endure a losing day.

Dunston Hall beckons on the way home: a steak and a nice bottle of the red stuff and all of a sudden the losing day doesn't seem so bad and tomorrow is another day.

It's also the time of year when I really do look forward to the Christmas festivities and try to keep myself busy since there is no racing for three days.

However, this means that I am really geared up for

the Boxing Day race cards and begin my homework early, so much so that nearly two weeks beforehand I believe I had found the winner of the King George Stakes.

Over the coming days the race card doesn't improve and I really struggle to find winners, or even decent each way bets. I receive some news that a new recruit to the Alan McCabe ranks, The Great Gabrial, is going to be pushed out to the front and finish ahead of the pack. I decide to spend the afternoon in the pub and write this:

We all meet at midday in Weatherspoon's and it's Guinness which is on the menu today. With Corals just across the road we are well set for the day. We pop in and back GABRIAL e/w at a great price of 12/1 and turning for home he is bolting along in the lead and I'm thinking we have all copped a nice one here.

Unfortunately, he doesn't quite last home and just gets run out of a place.

Apart from having a great afternoon with my friends, that race was the highlight of my day and it's a shame it did not win. The following day things are much better, except I have a cracking hangover, and I decide not to go racing again. I write this for my members:

It's very, very quiet this morning and I am really struggling to put anything up. As I say in my 11am email, I have been told that CYRIEN STAR is a very poor price at even money and it needs to be laid.

I commit the cardinal sin and pop into the local town to do some shopping and decide just to have a livener in the Swan Hotel. When I see Hilts is in there and shortly after Chappy arrives, I know I am on a slippery slope. Things don't get any better as Tony the Machine and Cabbage Paul arrive with the same idea as me for 'a quick livener'.

I have laid CYRIEN STAR for far too much at even money and am not in a position to put a lay-up in running, so I have to bite the bullet. Cabbage, the Machine and most of the Swan have backed around it. CYRIEN STAR is awful and never looks like winning and is soon tailed off and pulled up. All the boys have cleared up and I am glad I couldn't do a saviour and once again the black nectar is freely flowing.

My gardener arrives to pick me up, but nobody is in the mind to leave, but fortunately my one remaining brain cell kicks into action and reminds me I have Ascot tomorrow, so I drag myself away to the delight of my red hot credit card.

As I've said before information is key to successful betting so if you can't find it at the stables or on the gallops, then you'll have to find a trusted source online or from the Racing Post. On this particular day I head to Ascot and I'm amazed at the poor crowd. I tell my followers:

I am told that BABYMIX won't get a place today, so at 3/1, I lay this for the win and I also lay odds on that it won't get a place.

Venetia Williams is very sweet on the chances of her HOUBLON DES OBEAUX and at 7/2 I am told to make sure we all take this as it will shorten dramatically.

I also put up PADDYS SALTANTES under Adam Kirby at Lingfield e/w at 4/1.

Ascot is quieter than I can remember in past years and I am sure a lot of the bookmakers are also missing. In my opinion the bookmakers have made a rod for their own backs by being over-greedy and allowing the exchanges to take over. Also, if there was ever a power cut most of the books would be unable to form a market, without the exchanges and are certainly not brave enough to take them on.

BABY MIX sets a good gallop and is actually trading as fav at one point, but ultimately blows out and trails in unplaced, so a really nice winning start. Even better to come as HOUBLON really puts his head down and battles like a demon and wins at a very well backed 6/4. Ascot has been really kind to us today and we have absolutely cleaned up, which is always lovely just before the festive period.

Even Adam Kirby can't get Paddys home, although this is also smashed up in the betting from our 4/1 into 2/1 fav.

In summary, a pleasant drive home as we have made over 20 points profit + from our lay on BABYMIX.

The week actually ends with some very good news - Betfan have decided to switch my column from a Sunday to the incredibly popular Saturday newsletter which means that I should be able to provide better free tips for the readers. I am celebrating six months of tipping which I have enjoyed immensely; particularly since I have amassed more than 225 points in profit which means that anyone following me with a £10 stake has made £2,250 with me doing all of the work!

There are now three race-free days for me to cope with so I switch my computer off until Boxing Day morning and decide to do my Christmas shopping.

As I do every year, I don't have a list of potential presents to buy as such, I simply head to the shopping centre and buy what catches my eye. To make things easier, I also get the staff to wrap the presents which makes the whole thing a lot more bearable and saves me a tricky job that I'm not very good at.

It's probably best that I reprint my actual diary entry

from that day rather than trying to explain it!

Christmas Eve. I'm meeting the Great Alfonze at The Scole Inn (allegedly a favourite haunt of Dick Turpin) for our annual Christmas shopping jaunt and as usual he is running late, so time for an 8am swift pint of Guinness.

We arrive at the park and ride and get into the city for 9.30am.

The mall is always a good starting point as you can quickly knock 4 or 5 presents off your list quite rapidly. The Fonz is in pissed-off mode this morning and really not up for it, so I suggest a quick breakfast is in order, may be that will put some much needed life back into the geezer.

Breakfasts are fully consumed and a sweeping comment aimed at a portly lady's well-stocked plate with Alfonze stating he would rather feed her for a day than a week and once again the Great is back in the Alfonze.

The mall is now scoured for our loved one's goodies, with much more vigour.

Unfortunately, the lingerie shop assistants have wised-up nowadays and are not as gullible and forthcoming in puffing their assets when politely asked their size, as we think they're the same as our lady's!

The lists are getting gradually ticked off, but not without the odd steward's inquiry or two.

11am and our throats are like a camel driver's jock strap and after a quick directors' meeting we are in the Murders Pub, which even by our wayward standards is early and rather concerning. At £8 a glass, the Mulled wine is good and so it should be and after 4 each, walking down the avenue we are glowing as if we have just had the old Quaker Oats.

Shock horror!!! We are greeted by a not-so-smiley face in Debenhams and are quickly informed that Nora has retired and present wrapping is now not part of her job description, we are immediately put on the back foot and thinking what amount of Baileys could buy this red, round faced department store jobsworth? After the Great Alfonze has finished his impression of a man with Tourette's, we have more chance of a snowball in hell.

Plan B, finish our shopping as quickly as possible and head back to the Scole Inn and hope we can find a willing soldier.

I will never think picking the Grand National winner is difficult again as my choice of possible wrappers consists of an ex-Irish Tarmacker, a melon breasted barmaid, a drunken ex-school teacher, a bodyguard or a stroke victim.

Four pints of Guinness each later and it's now become apparent that we will have to do it ourselves. After a fashion and keeping the Fonz's shovel-like hands well away, the job is a good 'un. Parcels perfectly placed around the tree and time to chill before the big 'un tomorrow.

I have a really good Christmas Day with my family and friends but I'm also really touched to receive a number of Christmas wishes and thanks from subscribers and fellow tipsters. Now the pressure is back on, my phone is red hot once again and I write:

I am very surprised that on this huge day's racing the first phone call I get is from Fred at Newmarket telling me that all the faces are getting on ODIN in the 4.15 at Wolverhampton. I have no hesitation in putting this immediately out on my clients' emails and advising them to take 11/2 e/w and also telling them not to worry about the fact that it's not at one of the big meetings as a Wolverhampton winner buys as many groceries as a Kempton King George winner.

Amazingly my next bet is also out of Newmarket as I am told to back DUBAI PRINCE in the first at Kempton.

Biggles Steve is all over CLOUDY TOO and he is told it's expected to run a huge race at Wetherby today and the 3/1 looks a cracking price.

Finally, the Irish Hunter Chase boys are really up about the chances of TAMMYS HILL beating last year's top Hunter SALSIFY, so I have to put this up as well.

4 bets on the day and it all of a sudden seems as if we've never been away.

With regards to the King George, I private message all my clients that I think the ground has gone for DYNASTY and that I don't think CUE CARD will win, bold calls I know, but we have to be here to be shot at.

Not the perfect start as the Cheltenham-bound DUBAI PRINCE is shockingly disappointing and is eventually pulled up. When TAMMYS HILL beats Salsify all is still not well because ON THE FRINGE beats them both. The house seems more like a wake than a Boxing Day and surely all my clients are now boxing up their gifts ready for the pawn shop.

Phew, keep faith O great ones as CLOUDY TOO bolts up and all of a sudden we are nicely in profit and the Boxing Day jovialities can now begin with ODIN still to run at Wolverhampton.

Although we have no business done in the King George, I have made two very bold or stupid calls and even the turkey has to take second place as all eyes are on DYNASTY and CUE CARD.

DYNASTY never looks like troubling the scorers in all honesty, but the sprouts suddenly seem a tad hard as CUE CARD has not read the script AGAIN and is jumping for fun and pulling double.

How did CUE CARD get home last time over an extended 3 miles at Haydock still seems a mystery as he emptied out very quickly again today and is beaten into a distant 2nd.

'Georgie, Georgie Baker' rides a gem of a race on ODIN and all of a sudden the pawn shops are putting up the shutters, my fridge

is once again emptied of booze and I have called the King George correctly and WE have thrown another 20 points profit into the bin making December another ever-growing bookie bashing month with around 60 points profit.

Hilts is on his normal soap box and boring the pants of whoever is in earshot, when The Fonz isn't snoring he is as funny as ever, my father is his normal cool self, but his face the colour of the rising sun tells the whisky story. Sharon does her Weeble impression on the stairs and fails miserably as she lays in a heap at the bottom. Geoffrey 'ZZ top' the gardener is, well just out of it.

My granddaughter's father, Oliver is fast closing in on his second huuuuuu-bert toilet run, naughty Aunty Steph is teaching 2yo granddaughter Layla to do all things naughty, daughter Lauren is on the verge of drowning Oliver in his own sick and me - I am just Mr Sensible (LOL!).

The 20 points profit has put me at the top of the Betfan Christmas tree though, to be honest, I would prefer to be known as a star rather than a fairy! I'm a huge fan of the Dr Newland operation and my friend Biggles Steve, who manages to find information from somewhere, calls and asks what I have Act of Kalanisi tissued up as. I have it as 11/8 and we are amazed that he is trading at 15/8 so immediately pass the information on to my members. From what began as a very disappointing day is now looking very much brighter.

Not surprisingly, Act of Kalanisi does exactly what it says on the tin and leads the race all the way from the front, giving the Greedy Ones another Christmas bashing.

I am very happy that my Betfan column has been moved to a Saturday because I think I may tone down the bets on Sundays as its pretty dire stuff and most Sundays I struggle to find something.

Sundays should be a day for families and going out - not for studying crap form in rubbish races and if we haven't made our money during the week and are dependent or relying on Sundays, we need to hang up our Racing Posts and retire anyway.

Anyway, the pressure is back on and I'm keen to end the year on a winning streak. So far I have had six continuous winning days and I'm keen for a seventh. I top the Betfan league and put the effort in to find the winners I need - I end December with more than 100 points in profits! I am so relieved and proud of what I have done. Betfan really push my service and new members begin signing up which is pleasing; especially since I top the monthly and the three month tipster table and I'm second in the six month league tables. That's not bad for seven months of work!

I need to reassure readers and followers alike that I

won't be taking my finger off the pulse - indeed, I'm more determined to really top the table as the number one tipster on Betfan and be recognised further afield too. It's not easy work but I love horse racing and everything to do with it. I write this in my column:

With 2013 now finished and all the slates wiped clean, we need to start building our business together again and continue easing the cash out of the Greedy Ones. We have all got a nice tank and lots of ammo from our last year's excursions, as we made in excess of 280 points clear profit in our seven months together.

There's no free rides in this game and if any of us takes anything for granted or our fingers off the pulse or get complacent we will soon get bitten firmly on the arse and very quickly fall from grace.

Chapter 8

2014 begins well...

Thankfully, 2014 carries on where 2013 left off and I make it eight winning days. I then head to Huntingdon with Mr Jolly and I feel under pressure again to keep this winning streak rolling - if it's not one source of stress, it's another! Again, it feels very quiet at the course but I hear a whisper that Lucinda Russell's stable quietly fancies Happy River which is 6/1 - I advise a small e/w bet. I also tissue up a few others and advise those too. I write:

It's a fantastic sunny day and for once the A14 isn't very busy and it's a pleasure travelling up to Huntingdon with Mr Jolly and listening to his old time stories.

One story, he reminds me of, is when we were travelling back from Fakenham races in mid-winter and it was blowing a gale and pouring with rain.

We stopped at The Ram Inn for a drink on the way home, which turned into 4 or 5 (late homework again). We were about 4 miles from home on a tiny C road, when we noticed a tree had fallen across the high banks blocking the road, with alcohol-fuelled venom,

Mr Jolly stuck his toe down and went straight under the tree to an almighty bang and scratch on the roof, a blood curdling scream from Kenny in the front and somehow we've made it through. STOP, STOP NOW, Kenny screams and he was out of the car in a flash, only leaving the most awful smell inside (I will let you guess what had happened) refusing to get back in! Poor old Kenny walked (or squelched) the rest of his the way home.

I also receive some good news at the course and hear that Carobello who fell at Fakenham after a branch ripped through his muscle is not only on the road to recovery but is expected to race again. In the end I have a good result at Huntingdon and for my last tip I keep £50 for my drink and meal on the way home and put every penny I have on me on Caroles Destrier which goes on to win by 20 lengths.

The next day, as I was expecting, I write:

Right in the middle of our red hot winning streak and chasing the 10 winning days on the bounce, we are ruthlessly cut down in our prime with a bout of crap racing. Very unusual for a Friday, as it's normally quite busy. Let the Greedy Ones hang on to their booty for just one more day because I am certainly not going to start guessing or expecting any of you to back anything I am not prepared to back myself.

It's our second appearance tomorrow as the new Saturday Betfan face, so as long as this atrocious weather allows, we will see what tomorrow brings. As I said this morning in my clients' email, even with a day off, I am not going out with the boys as a detox is in order; don't panic! It will only be a matter of days, not weeks.

Sandown's card is already called off tomorrow and a lot of the jockeys are relocating to Wincanton, which I think is improbable, as when I called the clerk of the course today, he informed me that a lot of the racecourse is under water. Can you believe I am so bored today, I have no racing and I am sitting at home phoning clerk of the courses! This detox is in danger of only lasting a matter of hours, not even days.

Anyway, I needn't have worried since I did get back to winning ways! I write this for my readers:

The perfect Saturday yesterday, move over 'The Don' all my column readers got a really nice WINNING FREE tip, thanks to the battling qualities of DINGO BAY at 5/2 and my members and I made it an incredible 10 winning days on the trot, by tipping up and backing the Malcolm Jefferson trained RETREIVE THE STICK.

I thought we would wake up somewhere near the top of the Betfan tree this morning and we did, second, but miles behind Lord Howie, who had a rocket up his arse yesterday and hit a great double and very nearly an amazing treble.

Maybe Lord Howie needs to speak to our Kevin Deer AKA

the GMT for some advice on horse trebles, as whenever he's bored, he seems to keep hitting them with consummate ease.

Sundays, as I said, I am going to attempt to tone things down, but with information as strong as I've got today makes things very difficult. It's the Sussex National at Plumpton today and although it's not really my type of race, Biggles Steve really likes the chances of ADRENALIN FLIGHT at 7/1 e/w so I email this out and almost immediately after, I receive a call and am told that HANNAHS TURN is a 'good' thing today, so I immediately bet and email out a large stake on this as well.

As I said last week a detox was in order, I am beginning to think you have to be a monk or a fool to detox. When all your friends and associates get a sniff of this, they are absolutely no help whatsoever. I was only asking for a week-ish off it, goodness gracious surely that's not a crime. OK I admit, it was funny afterwards, but when the game local vicar turned up this morning at the front door clutching a case of Stella, courtesy of the boys from my local, it just makes one wonder a tad.

HANNAHS TURN although a drifter in the betting, our 'good thing' absolutely bolts up by an easy 7 lengths, so whatever happens later we have secured our 11th winning day on the trot.

ADRENALIN FLIGHT is never really going and is eventually pulled up in the bottomless ground.

Like I've said before, when things are going this well

and my confidence is up then the tipping just gets easier. Horses, literally, jump out of the cards demanding to be noticed. When I'm feeling this great I love going to the races and I write:

We have a really busy racing week ahead, as we are going to Leicester tomorrow, Wolverhampton Thursday to back what will be a short priced one, but I am assured it will win and finally Huntingdon on Friday - if the floods disperse.

The pressure is on again, it seems as if I am chasing an elusive winner not 12 winning days on the trot.

JAYEFF HERRING is working really well on the gallops in Newmarket for Michael Bell and they are confident of him making a winning handicap debut.

SUPERCILIARY is a good cracking e/w bet at 9/2 and although it's a 5th of the odds first 3, I think it's worth risking a small loss in the hope that we can secure a 9/2 winner.

The wily old Captain Alan Bailey scuppers us by beating JAYEFF HERRING and as I said SUPERCILIARY was a cracking e/w bet and it did exactly as we thought and did in fact get us only a place and that cemented our first losing day since the 20th of December.

The following day I lament:

It was inevitable that we were going to cop a losing day soon and yes finally, to the Greedy Ones' delight it happened yesterday.

We need to start all over again today and after such an incredible winning run as we all know we are now due a few losers, but we need to keep it to an absolute minimum and make sure we certainly don't give it all back, which we certainly WILL NOT.

Today I am putting out 2 e/w bets RENARD D'IRLANDE at 4/1 and MARCIANO 5/1 at Southwell.

I have caught the old rattler and on my way to Leicester racecourse, unfortunately Biggles is not going to be in attendance, as he has come up with a lame excuse, something about trimming his runway or some crap. So unless Hayley and the girls are out, it may end up being a quiet one.

On entering the course, I am horrified that I can't see the fish cart, so I can't have my habitual pint of jellied eels, good job one of the more jovial and human bookmakers is not in attendance, the larger than life Gary Wiltshire, because without his gallon of jellied eels the whole place would be in danger of being levelled.

I felt in a similar frame of mind, when for most of the way Venetia Williams's RENARD D'IRLAND jumps like a stag and is trading at odds-on, when he gets a rush of blood and takes off in Oakham and lands on top of the fence and shoots Aiden into the hurdles course.

Our fate is sealed, as is our second losing day when MARCIANO dwells at the stalls and can never quite make up the lost ground and just misses out on a place. Time to get out of here.

*Can you believe there are a million taxis at the station buzzing around like flies at a sh*t bucket and not a single unbooked one at the races? I am lucky enough that my sweet smile allows me to slip into one with a very nice elderly couple. I invite my co-pilots to the Slug and Lettuce, but hardly surprisingly they decline.*

It's relative quiet and bearing in mind I am 'Billy No Mates' at the moment, I decide to see whether Yates is any better. It is a bit but not mind blowing, maybe it's me after enduring my second losing day, but I do decide to just try The Kings Head before I endure the boring journey home. No Hayley, no Miss Sweden = NO FUN.

Gloom and doom, on the train home, armed with no winners, stories or jovialities. Don't worry I'm not quite at the stage of jacking it all in to go shelf stacking quite yet.

Not surprisingly I begin to become cautious with my tips and tone things down a shade. One of the biggest things in professional punting is to know when to upsize and downsize your bets and after such an incredible winning run and then the almost inevitable two losing days, it's time just to be level-headed.

I put up a small e/w bet on ROXY LANE at 8/1, as this has a profile of a horse that has been laid out for a gamble and I hope today is the day my luck changes. It doesn't.

What can I say? ROXY LANE is stone cold bollock last, what a joke tip, I hope for all the owners' sake, I was wrong and today wasn't meant to be the day.

*I am doing nothing different to what I did for our winning run and I am not going to attempt to hide it, as I do love to write about and enjoy the winning ones, I have to be consistent in these emotions because anybody that says they win all the time (I'm not saying make consistent profits, because we do), take a long look at them and just think you are full of sh*t.*

Then I'm hit with a conundrum. I know I have to be more careful but like most gamblers I have an urge to find that winning streak again but I then receive information that is so strong that I really want to smash the bookies with it. I decide to crank things up, but not full bore, as I have made more than 200 points in under three months and only had three losing days on the trot.

To my mind, I have nothing to prove - the winning days will return. I write:

I am going to Wolverhampton racing today, as I also have some business there which will benefit us in the future and I am also going to hammer BIG BAZ in the 4.40.

I email my ever-growing client list at 8am, with BIG BAZ, as I think 13/8 is an incredible price for a horse, which I am told WILL win today and then will go on to contest NH bumpers. Normally, I would put him out as a MAXIMUM bet, but I do curb my enthusiasm a shade.

An hour into my journey, I am told that BIG BAZ is now trading at odds-on, so I decide to rearrange my meeting and re-route to Billericay to meet Smudger and Irish Pete.

On arrival at Smudger's, I quickly email out the rest of my selections for the day, rather later than normal due to the A12.

The 2.20 Southwell, Fred from Newmarket informs me that all the right money and faces are backing PETES FRIEND, so at 5/2, this is our first runner. 2.35 and Biggles Steve is told that CHAC DU CADRAN is thought to be back to his best and at 9/2 we back him e/w.

I am very conscious that we have already had a really big bet on Big Baz at 13/8 and we have now added two more to our betting slips.

I know it's easy for me just to keep emailing bets through with points attached, bearing in mind it's real money and livelihoods I am dealing with, also I am personally backing all these, so my conscience decides for me to forsake my gain of Betfan points, although I am told it's expected to win and give Magic Skyline as a free bet on the bottom of my email.

We settle in front of the TV to watch the racing around Smudger's table and Pete has just about devoured his second sandwich as McCoy kicks Magic Skyline in the Bellie and we're off.

Four minutes later and we have landed our first winner of the day as Magic Skyline is never in a moment's doubt as he bolts in by 14 lengths and all our Betfair and Betdaq accounts look much healthier.

We have hardly finished congratulating ourselves and I get some very HOT, HOT late information that Tony McCoy on board Getabuz is also expected to win the next as well. You can imagine three blokes egging each other on, we all press up on Getabuz at 3/1 and 11/4 and amazingly another four minutes later, we are all high fiving around the table as this bolts in by nine lengths.

I can't take the credit for this one, as Smudger reads the column as well, he gets a call from a trusted contact telling him that Maakirr has just been punted by a very well respected person, so once again we all pile in, but I must admit I am rather more careful but Maakirr wins by a neck! This is unbelievable and is now in danger of being a 10 pint pub story.

Our second bet, Peters Friend, misses the break and I think that's just typical! My biggest bet so far today, my first members bet proper and we are trailing in last and trading at 10/1 in running. Amazingly Peters Friend and Royal Holiday flash past the post together and we can't call it, Oi Oi Peters Friend gets it. We have all had four winning bets on the trot, a script you couldn't write.

Chac du Cadran is our first loser of the day and at 9/2 no real damage done, but nevertheless a loser.

Time to head our separate ways, Peter has eaten Smudger out of bread and ham and smoked himself half to death, but after his divvy-up he has won well over £1,000! I have drunk far too many cups of tea, yes tea, and worn a path to the loo and after our respective roll calls, Smudger and I make the day's total winnings up to nearly £6,000. With Big Baz still to run.

I stagger my journey home and stop at my father's to watch Big Baz run. Unbelievably, it's trading at 2s-on and because I've had an incredible day, I press up on my early 13/8. He wins with his head firmly in his chest and that rounds off a day to remember, especially after three losing days on the trot.

That's a cool 17 point winning day, plus a free winner

chucked in for good measure to the Betfan newsletter readers.

In the days that come, I get into a battle with fellow Betfan tipster Simon Holden and we have a 'showdown' on the Saturday. I win 40 points with 4/1, 11/4 and 4/5 winners. I also had a Trixie bet which had two winners and a second which could have been another 50 points. Unfortunately, despite this great performance, Holden manages to do better than me and I congratulate him and his performance in the newsletter (through gritted teeth!).

In addition to visiting the country's racecourses on a regular basis I also use my winnings to go on several holidays a year. January is a good time to find some sun and it's paid for by Corals. After a relaxing break which saw me make a profit on the pre-bought drinks package (£300 - that's two days drinking for me!) and I did a daily 'Man vs Food' challenge to really enjoy myself.

I come home and head to the Newmarket gallops and get some decent information which will pay for my May holiday in Malta. The good news is that I return to my winning ways. Indeed, it's like I've never been away and I write:

The phones have all been red hot today and I think for a

Tuesday we have some exciting information.

I am told that today is the day for a touch on COOL GEORGE, who is trading at 13/2 and will not be out of the 3, barring accidents of course and is expected to go very close. I get Smudger and Chippy Pete to back this for me at 13/2 and 6/1 and email this out immediately, as the story I'm told makes full sense and I can relate to.

NO WIN NO FEE is in receipt of 6lb from the fav for only 1/2 a length beating and looks a great e/w bet at 5/1, although we have to factor that into the price as we are backing apprentices.

I've been having my double garage converted into a flat and having an office built above it, so it's the day to pick a couple of flat screen TV's to grace the walls, so I can have channels 415 and 432 on at the same time. Pathetic isn't it? Can't even turn the one television over nowadays, we have to have two.

TV's sorted is the easy bit as we now need to lug the pool table and juke box up there.

Jumping two out COOL GEORGE is trading at 1/10 in running and has apparently paid for my cruise and both of the flat screens, in my ignorance, I don't even notice McCoy coming until it's evident his persistence has paid off and he does us after the last on the run-in. Damn and blast or something not similar, a small profit, but I am gutted.

NO WIN NO FEE doesn't help my mood as our local boy Louis Steward causes a knock on effect, which totally destroys any chance we ever had of even getting a place.

A losing day which could so easily of been a very good winning one, but hey tomorrow's another day.

The following day and the information keeps coming and I'm told about eight different horses. I do the homework and they all look like great prospects - so I decide to put them all up. It's not an easy decision and I'm racked with worry as soon as I decide to do it. In addition, my final bet of the day is a 10 point e/w Trixie. I must be mad and write:

I am well aware that I have put out a lot of points/monies today and it's a great deal of points/monies to be found and laid out, not only for you, but also myself.

I do take solace in the fact that we are nearly 50 points up this month, won over 100 points in December and over 80ish in November, so if it does go tits up today, I do have a small, very small hiding place and I can hopefully beg forgiveness.

With that all over, I need to pop out and have a quick clothing update, a new pair of Converse trainers or shoes, I don't know what they're called, some very loose fitting T-shirts and some 3/4 jeans, an elastic waist is a must for the upcoming cruise.

Thankfully, the first tip bolts up as expected and it's a

cracking start to the day - and some of the pressure is off. In the next, I'm thinking this is our second winner of the day two furlongs out, as he's cruising along and both in front are being pushed, unfortunately he flatters to deceive and doesn't find on the heavy ground and finishes third. A losing single win bet, but we are still going in our e/w Trixie.

My third is taken on for the lead and it's 'good night nurse' to our 5/2 and I am left wishing I had laid all my bets off, Mmmmm hindsight! If we could bottle it we would all be millionaires.

The next doesn't start well and is trailing at the back of the field and I am thinking it needs 7lb off its back and not on it and counting our losses on the e/w single and also the e/w Trixie when, all of a sudden, the very green running little 4-year-old filly gets the idea and flies up the outside and takes the lead, although she runs very green in front she still does it! A nice winner at 11/2. In the end I made about 30 points in profit for my members. A good day all round.

This is also an interesting week because, finally, I begin a late tipping service. I mentioned previously about being at the course and getting a piece of information that would prove useful so I'm now going to put it into practice. This information was being received after I had done all of my emails which means winners are slipping through the net. In addition to the 70 odd points I have racked up this month, my proofing has proved there is a lot more mileage and money to be earned from this late information service, as this is already 46 points up this month and over 110 points up in just over two months.

All these tips are totally different to my main tipping line. The only thing I must do is to get the information out to subscribers at least an hour before the off. Obviously, there won't be a tip every day but I assume it will average out at around four or five a week to start with.

The winter weather depresses me so I head to sunnier climes and send out a column at 4am! I write:

Right an early start this morning, I am getting my column bang up-to-date at 4am, as leaving for Luton airport at 5.30am to fly to Santa Cruz. I'm not a great flyer, but I hasten to add, much better than I used to be, when I had to have a head band over my eyes, only removing it to consume more of the old Mother-in-law's ruin or stagger to the Thomas crapper.

I still have to have more than a few liveners to get on the smartie pot, but flying is now bearable and a must to enjoy the extra spoils of our gains. I must admit, I wasn't at my best in the early stages of my adult travelling career, when my father nudged me to lift my head band to introduce me to his very good Maltese friend, a *very pleasant man until I realised it was the f*****g captain and screamed: "Who's flying this b*****d thing?"*

Even though I'm enjoying the cruise I'm still working on finding winners for my members. Also, I advise that a good tip on a cruise is to tip the staff, especially waiters, on the first night and not at the end as you won't get the 'extras'.

This pays off handsomely for me since the all-inclusive wine is just awful but after bunging Benjamin the waiter a big wad in his top pocket he soon brings me a different bottle to everyone else and it's very much nicer.

I also put Benjamin right about the 'posh portions' being dished up and make clear I'm a big lad with a big appetite.

The only downside is there isn't free wifi on board (£18 for three hours? The jokers!) so I struggle as best I can and go ashore to find a better signal whenever possible. I find some winners, have a losing day or two, I find a couple of interesting e/w tips and write:

I also decide that these two will make a very good 3pt e/w double at 5/2 and 15/8. I know a lot of people think, what's that prat doing today, two shorties and an e/w double? In my defence, if we cop it's a real nice return of 30ish points and also backing these singularly, a total loss is difficult to envisage.

Although we have a great day a sea today, what I'm going to tell you now, made me bend double with laughter.

My dad, bless him, was sitting on deck 9 at the front letting the world slip by with his JB whiskey in one hand and his iPad in the other, with his ear plugs in.

As I got closer, I could see all around him that these poshies were all looking and frowning in his general direction and there was quite a manly gathering also, OMG, I soon knew why, I could hear his iPad screaming out either Jimmy Jones or Jim Davidson, whoever it was, "f" this and "f" that and the odd C U Next Tuesday as he sat there blissfully unaware he hadn't pushed his earplugs in completely and he was entertaining the whole front deck, well a large majority of it anyway.

Back home and the Betfan tipsters are getting bolshie and want another Saturday showdown. I'm still in the sunshine, though there's an outbreak of illness which means the bars and restaurants become quieter, but I'm game for it.

We finally get home through very rough waves and cold weather and I'm soon back to business.

Chapter 9

One of my greatest days

February begins with a small loss but I'm unconcerned because I'm confident about the day's racing - it might be a Sunday but I know my contacts have something for me. I write:

It is Hunter Chaser day again today and we are just waiting for our contact to walk the course and get back to us.

Fred is on the mobile telling me that BROUGHTON has really blossomed since his last run and has been galloping and schooling with previous winners and going just as well. The ground will suit and if he transforms his homework to the track today he is fully expected to win and secure his ticket to the Cheltenham Festival in March. At 13/8 knowing this price will soon disappear, I email out and also back myself.

The news comes from the track that we have been waiting for, all systems go.

THATS RHYTHAM is the boy we are backing today. Page who has won on the old boy the last twice and rides him in all his homework is once again on board.

We are told not to be put off by RHYTHAM now being 14 years old as he is as good as ever. I email this out as an e/w bet at

15/2 with Victor Chandler and as soon as I have done this it goes 8/1, which I am not overly concerned about because they are 'best odds guaranteed'. Also better known as my 'prat's bet', I put them both in an e/w double.

Right all done, now out to Sunday lunch at the local and as I have invited the whole tribe over today, I hope we can cop a winner, because odds-on the bill is already in my corner.

The Sunday lunch is OK, but as always it could be done better at home, how often do we say that? I am not the greatest fan of Aunt Bessies Yorkshire puds, rubbery crap, how long does it take to whip up a bit of flour, eggs and milk? The red vino is really good and there's no clearing up so it's worth it.

I sneak into the bar to listen to BROUGHTON and never get over-excited because it sounds very much like what I was told this morning; a cake walk and at odds-on as well, so a great start to the day. We have already multiplied our monies by about 10ish times and have made a profit on the day already.

Now we have our big e/w bet looming on THATS RYTHAM and also the icing on the cake, the prat's e/w double.

I now have an hour and a half to kill and although I'm in the boozer, I bet this is going to drag on as I MUST be home to watch our Hunter bet.

It's the bum's rush time for the lingering family now, as getting home for the 4.00 is a must.

I am amazed to see our charge has slipped out to an

incredible 12/1. Page has him nicely settled on the outside and out of troubles way for the first circuit, where the second fav falls. Three out and the family and I begin to get more animated as we move into third on the inside and as we jump two out the whole of Jafeica House erupts into raptures of 'come on's' and jumping the last it's screams and 'oi oi's' and believe me it's the longest furlong I can remember for a long time. OI OI, WE HAVE DONE IT, both our bets have won nicely and we have also won our e/w double.

During the bedlam I have a quick count-up and think we have all multiplied our preferred stakes by over 100 times.

Although them Greedy Ones have somehow nicked a point off us, as it was 12s on the off and has been returned at 11s.

As you know news travels fast and the mobile is red hot, the Great Alfonze is soon on his way over, Hilts knows because he has put a cash bet on for me so he is winging his way over and with the most of the crew already present, I can see this being a late one and the Jafeica House wine reserves getting severely hit.

It really was a great day for tipping and one of those moments you wish everyone in the world knew what you could do. I write:

No prizes for guessing we didn't finish our jolly-up until far too late and the bottles are living proof that too much was consumed by all. It's like the day after the Lord Mayor's show here and also the day's racing has a similar look.

We are now already 106 points in profit for February, to go with our 100+ points profits in January and December with just a poultry 80+ in November heheheh cocky bastard.

I think it prudent just to send out a little calming and feet back on the ground email as soon as I've gathered myself, just saying please don't just give all our winnings back like mug punters, which we certainly are not and to stick to suggested stakes and not up them just at the moment.

It's 11am and nothing strong enough to tempt us has come through or shown up on my figures or tissues, I know we are all gagging to get stuck in again today, but I suggest we all sit on our hands and keep our powder dry for later in the week.

I have to collect a cash bet from one of the two local Corals, so I pop out with Tony the Machine to collect it. As I collect yesterday's small bet and large winnings, I can tell my betting days in here are also now numbered.

Just as we enter Weatherspoon's to spend good old Joes money again, I get a call regarding the stayer WAVING in the 2.40 at Wolverhampton.

When this guy calls I really take notice and as it's too late for my main ANDY BELL service so I email and text this out to my LATE BETTING SERVICE and advise taking the 11/10 on show. As we have two Corals within walking distance we descend upon the other and reinvest Joe's own cash in his other shop.

With 45 minutes to spare we have time for that pint before the race, which is ultimately two. Having taken 5/4 in the shop, coming round the top bend WAVING comes trotting round the outside and just 'waves' goodbye to the rest and wins easily. That's the beer money sorted for the day or rather the week and Joe gets hit with double bubble.

A nice winning day for the LATE service and all my ANDY BELL clients didn't have to sit on their hands all day, as I know a lot of you are members of both services.

With the Cheltenham Festival on the horizon, my favourite event in racing's calendar, I'm really enthusiastic about my prospects. Then I get a call from Betfan asking if I would be interested in a grudge match with another top tipster, the Gambling Don (or, as I continually call him 'the Grumbling Don' because this bloke never stops moaning). I tell the chiefs that I would be interested - mainly because it's a great opportunity to get one over on him.

The month continues to go really well, I'm more than 100 points in profits, and the winners just keep on coming. I decide to go to Huntingdon but the weather is appalling and I'm surprised it hasn't been called off. I write:

The journey to Huntingdon is horrendous with the constant spray on the windscreen and the ever pulling out lorries halting the traffic flow.

Mr Jolly's well told and rehearsed story does cheer me up, which was about the time when Michael Chapman (still my neighbour) and myself left our local The Grapes to walk to The Swan, passing his house in the process on Christmas eve, after a long afternoon, as good Samaritans do, we knocked on Mr Jolly's door to see if he wanted to join us this Christmas Eve, more probably to bum a lift and after a few knocks and no answer we went in and called as we thought he was asleep.

Still no answer. What a fantastic smell was wafting from the oven in the kitchen, full of Dutch courage, we had to inspect. Wow a fantastic plump, cooked turkey.

Just a quick taste later and the bones were ready for the next day's soup boiling. Heheheh we waddled down to the Swan and kept our ill-gotten booty story all to ourselves. I wish we could have witnessed and pictured Mr Jolly's face the next morning getting his turkey out to put the roasties in and being presented with well-sucked bones.

How awful, but as they say all good comes out of bad as his neighbour Paul 'Potty' Potter invited him for Christmas lunch and he has done to this day, 30 years on.

The Venetia Williams mudlark bolts up in the first as it does in the second, whatever am I doing taking her on, what a bad error of judgement. I even ask her how she does it in the owners' and trainers' bar and with a wry smile she replies 'must be magic!'

RETREIVE travels really well and looks the most likely winner two out and just runs out of steam as it did last time, personally I don't think this is going to be a lot of good and will be found another job.

The only thing that brightens up my day is being told the Nicholls hotpot BLACK RIVER is very ponderous and can't jump at home, so I lay him at 6/4ish on Betdaq to regain a few losses.

The rain continues to fall which I hate to see because it makes finding winners much more difficult.

Over the coming weeks the contest between myself and the 'Grumbling Don' continues to ramp up and he then throws down a challenge of a £5,000 wager to the best tipster at the Cheltenham Festival. Far from being put off, it only gives me more of an incentive.

It doesn't help that he keeps banging on about being Betfan's 'number one all-time tipster' which is rather like Lester Piggott claiming he could beat Richard Hughes in a race today. I don't think so.

Meanwhile, I continued my good run of form and my new late betting service also begins knocking in well priced winners, despite the horrendous and inclement weather. In the middle of February, I'm topping the tipsters' table and my new service is quickly rolling in at fourth place with a 50% strike rate. I write this:

Jumping on the 10.07 train to Leicester today, thank goodness it's on and I can get out again.

I arrive at Leicester to the disappointing news that our big Hunter Chaser bet is not happening today as the ground is verging on being heavy. Although all is not doom and gloom as I am told that BIN END in the 2.40 which is trading at 7/2, I am rather cautious as the conditions here today are awful and back and advise this as an e/w chance.

Venetia Williams kicks off with her now habitual first winner of the day and the David Bridgewater connections are confidently smashing up their Don't Do Mondays in the second and, how often does this happen, David Bridgewater wins with his other un-backed horse. There are a lot of glum faces in the owners' and trainers' bar afterwards and I think there will be questions asked.

The Grumbling Don is creeping around the paddock and I can't resist getting into his ribs about our Cheltenham side bet, which is met with a 'good luck boy' through gritted teeth. Maybe his bravado or the boss Penny (his wife) has caught up with him, as he couldn't hardly raise a smile and sloped off.

I have a Grumbling Don face on after BIN END is brought down at the very first and the journey home is looking more daunting than ever. I get some comfort food - jellied eels - in hope they will stimulate the brain in this now driving snow.

The Hunter Chase goes without any great surprises apart from a 50/1 shot nearly nicking it coming up the hill and making the very confident SHY JOHN jockey look very silly.

We have logged another losing day, a mind blowing two on the trot now and I am freezing cold and have got a four hour journey home, with only Fakenham to look forward to tomorrow. Wow another cold and wet one.

Despite the early starts and the legwork I have to put in to find winners, I still love going to the courses - even in the depths of winter. Like I say I love everything about horse racing and try to support it whenever I can. I write this in my column:

For once I wouldn't be overly-concerned if Fakenham was called off, as it's renowned for being the coldest course in the country and today, already the rain is teaming down and the wind is howling.

I know if I cry off I will be letting Mr Jolly down, come rain or shine he always looks forward to his days out, which are unfortunately numbered now and that always helps to keep me motivated on days like these.

I decide as the prices are very cramped and small fields, to put up a win Trixie, which includes SPIRIT OSCAR in the second at 5/4, MISTRAL REINE at 7/4 and finally and certainly not least DOCTOR HARPER, which is the strongest and my banker of the day.

As always the cart tracks to Fakenham are awful and it takes just under two hours to get there.

SPIRIT OSCAR never really jumps and when he hits three out it seals his fate or rather defeat and that isn't the start that I or any of us wanted.

The owners' and trainers' bar is heaving, which isn't difficult as it's rather like your Grandmother's living room anyway, also it's like your Grandmother behind the counter, although she is lovely.

What's happening to me? My first bet is second, it's raining, it's windy and it is The Grumbler himself hoovering up all the sandwiches and cakes, I find myself wondering how many has he tucked away in his coat pockets for later. (Probably Penny's Valentine's meal).

Granny does make me a lovely cup of tea which is most appreciated. The Don calls me over but I make my excuses in favour of the elements and the paddock.

MISTRAL REINE is always well placed on the outside

where the better ground appears to be and when Leighton shakes the reins the race is all over as he pulls away and wins very easily to kick off our Trixie.

Mr Jolly is in need of a warming as the heaters on his wheelchair don't seem to be working. I take him to the owners' bar for a cuppa and Mr Grumbling is waiting.

As I'm now in a more positive frame of mind after a winner, I do ask the Don what he's doing in these parts, apparently he is here to back SAFFRON WELLS, which he has been told will win from his Newmarket connections.

Typical, I think, I need DOCTOR HARPER to show all my members a profit on the day and I have also just put ALL my cash on it at an amazing price of 5/4. The Don goes into great lengths to why his fancy can win, I just can't see it, as I tell him I have The DOCTOR tissued up a 1/2 on, because he is 23lbs well in and even after all the allowances he is still 16lbs well in. I do now have a niggle in my mind as to why the DOCTOR has drifted to such a big price of 5/4, but hey hoe too late now Bellie Boy I think as I'm already all in.

Oi Oi DOCTOR HARPER is never challenged and leads all the way to give us a double in our Trixie and a winning day. The rain and wind doesn't seem so bad now as I am waiting at the bookies to draw my winnings, all in CASH heheheh. I don't look for The Don on my way out as it's not P.C. to gloat.

Winning days are back again and we were unlucky that we

didn't cop all 3 winners, instead of 2 winners and a second, which would have been so much more profitable.

I get home just in time to watch our LATE BETTING SERVICE horse LOUIS VEE, which we have backed at 7/4 for good money, totally miss the break and trail the field for half the race, until he decides to pick up the bridle and wins going away. So another nice winning day for all the LATE BETTING service boys and girls.

The weather might be poor but my spirits were lifted by a good day at Fakenham and I top the table with my late service coming second. The only cloud for me is that I'm increasingly concerned that many of the horses racing now in heavy conditions may not recover in time for Cheltenham so the picking of winners is getting more difficult with every passing day. Having said that, in the coming days I post a few ante-post bets out to my members. The weather doesn't pick up and I write this:

The cards look very ordinary this morning and things seem to be very quiet on all fronts as well. I think we will get a few days like this as all attention and thoughts will now be slowly switching to Cheltenham.

I decide at lunchtime as nothing has materialised to make

my way up to Leicester for tomorrow's racing so I can be nice and fresh and make an early start. Just as I am nearing the A6, I finally get a call regarding a 'must' bet at Wolverhampton later this afternoon. In the 5.00 ARANTES who is trained by the ex-Canary Mick Channon is trading at 5/4, but I am told he is expected to win. Also during the same call I am told that SHAN VALLEY will go close, but to have a smaller bet on her. I stop at Burger King on the A6 and email these both out to the LATE BETTING service.

I find my pre-booked hotel, just off London Road, which is on the racecourse side of the town and on entry I am greeted by one of the locals, an Indian, a very nice chap, who is in the process of lightening my credit card, when I realise there is no internet. The card is very quickly withdrawn from the machine and he is told the card is not working until the internet is.

This little 5ft man has now turned his back and is screaming in the backroom direction, maybe he is ordering me a curry or a hit squad because I have absolutely no idea. Amazingly a ladder and two gofers quickly appear and just as quickly disappear upstairs and into a cupboard, as cool as a cucumber, as if nothing has happened, he says, "Just one minute, sir."

With another quick unfamiliar unLeicestershire bark and my bag and I and my still intact credit card are being ushered upstairs. I obviously have the ex-headmaster's room at the top of this converted old school house which is very nice, clean, big shower room and a big flat screen TV.

I quickly dump my stuff and hail a cab to the nearest bookies, just in time to see SHAN VALLEY pulling and jumping like a cow, in her defence she picks up the bridle and battles all the way home and finishes a creditable second, without her early race antics, I think she would have won. ARANTES is visually the winner two furlongs from home and doesn't disappoint and wins easily at odds-on, which makes our 5/4 look very juicy indeed.

Room and journey paid for, the job and the day's a good 'un. Quick shower and spruce up, a meeting with Biggles Steve is already planned and let's see what Leicester's made of.

I then spend a few days 'on the road' in Leicester and Newmarket and then head home to work on the Cheltenham card. Again. I'm still knocking in small profits but the late service is now beating my main service which, surprisingly, pleases me. I must confess too that a lot of people envy my lifestyle and quite a few don't but after a few days away of beer, restaurants, racecourses, gambling and clubs, I really do enjoy the creature comforts of home. There's a homely fire, meat and two veg meals and lovely wine to enjoy. Then I'm back on the road again and I write:

It's the 10.17 train to Doncaster today and that tart

'Olivier' Holden, or is it Hardy?, can't come because he's in the recording studios at Betfan 'Hollywood' Towers; let's hope the launderette ladies felt sorry for us lot watching his promo video last week and chucked some of their black and white knickers in the wash to negate that tanny colour on his Primarny suit.

My tissues, the form sheets and the masses of contacts have once again drawn a blank on the last day of February.

Doncaster is relatively quiet today, not only on the bets front, but also the head count and no shenanigans today or tonight to be reported, as I am heading home, on the correct timed train I hasten to add.

On the rattler home now, the correct one. I don't think there was a great deal to be learned from today's racing and I am glad we didn't have a bet.

Not a great month for my service after a cracking start, but we did ultimately finish in profit, although it was well below par. Let's get the blips and hard luck stories out of the way before the real fun starts in 11 days. I was very pleased with THE LATE BETTING service which ended the month with over 60 points profit. It will be a very interesting service for Cheltenham and could easily fly, when a lot of the cards are played late and an awful lot can be learned and picked up from the betting ring.

So the month disappoints and I have a major festival

lined up - the greatest steeple chasing month in the calendar. I have increased the already massive pressure upon myself by taking the Grumbling Don on over the four days and making a selection in every race.

In the heat of the moment these side bets are great fun to agree to but as I trawl through the cards, I realise the task is going to be very difficult. I'm sure on the day I will step up and make a real go of it and show the doubters that I am one of the country's best tipsters.

Chapter 10

The lull before the storm...

Just typical - as soon as my column moves to the more popular Saturday slot from the Sunday, I'm suddenly knocking in winners on a Sunday! However, my free tips don't always shine and I confess that only one in three or four goes on to win. I think this is because I change my selection strategy to impress and I want the bigger prices to win for myself and the readers. At this point I decide to go back to basics for the freebies and be more realistic. I tell readers:

If the shrewd Dessy Hughes thinks ART OF PAYROLL warrants a county hurdle entry and he needs a few more pounds to give him a chance of getting in, then surely today is his final chance of a ticket there. He is going to be bang up for today's challenge and should show these a clean set of heals. At 7/4 I email out this information and advise taking the price.

When I was at Leicester three weeks ago and we backed BIN END, if you can remember and yes it was the 13th, he was unfortunately brought down at the first, but our second choice today ran in the very same race TOKIO JAVILEX.

It was his chasing debut and he was a very impressive second, so maybe some good can come out of the 13th's race and we can recoup our losses today at a short price of 5/4.

I personally back these and also advise the same, backing both of these in win singles and also in a win double.

Today it's lunch at the boozer and a nice bottle of vino and hopefully I shall return home to some nice news this evening when I look at the results.

Obviously both of the tips were good winners! The results push us up the Betfan tipster tree. The next few days go well and I'm feeling great what with Cheltenham on the horizon and my huge challenge with the Grumbling Don.

It's not all fun and games doing what I do, travelling the country for race meetings and I write:

I'm not looking forward to today whatsoever, I am visiting my very good racing friend Ken, who I have written about many times in my after-racing Yarmouth jolly jaunts. The awful Big C has got its claws into him and he is currently in the Norfolk and Norwich Hospital. I am picking up our very good friend and landlady of the Colonel H in Yarmouth, Ruth.

My concentration isn't great today, so I am pleased when I get a call from the Appleby stable saying they fancy spoiling the STAND GUARD party today by beating him with their STAFF SERGEANT.

Ruth and I have a couple of drinks before we visit Ken, which isn't always the most sensible idea, as it does tend to bring the emotions to the fore quicker.

The mood of the day isn't helped by having no winners but then that's how it goes. Things don't really improve because the racing is usually quite poor with a big festival coming up but I manage to find some winners among the dross. This translates into more pressure for me and I write:

I am up to my eyeballs in form books, printed sheets, papers and the old faithful Weatherbys betting guide this morning. I am really going to start cracking up the heat with the Grumbling Don today, in my attempt to not only beat him and the bookies, but to ensure we all have a very successful and prosperous Festival. The ground seems to be drying out very nicely, which as a rule of the thumb normally suits the more fancied runners. I can see that "THE ROCK HOLDEN" is now sitting firmly on the fence with regards to my and the Don's challenge.

It doesn't seem as though we have been setting the world alight yet this month on the tipping front, but looking at the figures, we are still hitting an amazing 54% winners and are nicely in profit for March.

I am on the 10.07 train to Leicester this morning and it's the last journey out until the big one into Shakespeare's county on Monday and his theatre is not part of the itinerary.

Leicester was meant to be a good earner today, but shortly after arriving I am told that the ground hasn't dried enough to be sure enough of putting our monies down. I shall watch just a couple of races and then head home to get some more work done on Cheltenham.

I think next week's column will be a must read, as things are already starting to simmer to boiling point. I have SIX great bets lined-up already, the first of which is already winging its way towards the Grumbling Don's corner and sticking it up him at a juicy price of 20/1.

This time next week all the talking will be over and one of us will be £5,000 richer. I am very impressed with the interest the challenge has generated and the vast number of people that have also put their monies where their mouths are and signed up.

The challenge will be unique and by no means easy as we have agreed to pick a horse in every race of every day, so there will be no hiding place until the flag is finally lifted on the Grand Annual on Friday evening and by this time everybody that has had the good foresight to sign up to my service will have had access to 12-14 top selections a day, around 50 on the week, which will equate to around a poultry 60p a selection.

Win or lose Bellie Boy, the one certainty is next week's

column is going to be..... Mmmmm "Interesting".

The following day I inform my readers:

What a disaster yesterday was, I think with all my selections I only beat about 4 horses all day, so I don't think we will dwell on what happened and quickly move on.

I thought I had seen and moved enough crap this morning when I finished cleaning our chicken shed out, but far from it - there was way more in the Grumbling's column this morning.

We are taking the Hunter Chase route today and backing ROB CONTI and GOLAN WAY both singularly and in a win double. I haven't got much planned today, no going out for Sunday lunch and wine as this coming week my digestive system is going to be abused with a poor diet and a great intake of alcohol.

I mentioned previously that a lot of tipping needs confidence and when things don't go well it really shakes my belief. Everyone suffers and you just have to get past it. I don't appreciate the stress and trouble that Cheltenham will bring and start praying that the whole Festival will be a good one for me. Then on the Monday, I write:

All today's roads lead to Cheltenham or rather tracks as I am catching 10.24 train and arriving at 3.01. I have arranged to meet "The Rock Holden" in the coffee shop opposite the station and then on to our flat, where we are staying for the week. Manchester Pete is arriving at tea time and the week's crew is then complete.

As I have only a few finishing touches to complete tomorrow's cards, we decide to pop into town for a swifty. We have our first festival drink in the Montpelier wine bar, which for a Monday night is packed, so we move onto O'Neill's just across the road and this is heaving too. After two pints of the Black Nectar we wander down the street to more tranquil surroundings and relax with a nice bottle of white wine and a red in the Queen's Hotel.

The following day and I'm like a little kid on Christmas morning. I get the work done and then prepare for the great day's racing. I write:

The form is done, all my selections are sent and the moment of the first race roar we have all been waiting for is very nearly upon us. As I receive confirmation of the competition's selections, I am quietly confident of kicking The Don's arse today, as I can't see where he is coming from on three of his.

We are in front of the rails bookmakers as the first race begins and the roar is tremendous and the tingle goes through your body and all of a sudden the talking is over.

Tony McCoy is cruising through the field when he smashes the third last on GILGAMBOA and that his, and our, race over with. Not the dream start, but 27 races left so no concerns yet.

We pitch up in the Miller bar and have a stomach settling Guinness. TRIFOLIUM looks terrific in the paddock and I am sure we will get a place and very hopeful of nicking it. I manage to get 9/2 on the rails and turning for home I am thinking we can win this, very gallant in defeat and not quite good enough on the day, but a very small profit gained personally and a wash through on the competition.

The big Irish contingent are bemused, as I am, by how poorly WRONG TURN runs, I can only put it down to the ground being too quick for him. The Don gets his day going with a 25/1 place and has his nose in front.

My nap of the day JETZI is next, I have piled into this big time e/w at 10/1 as I have huge negatives for the front three, HURRICANE FLY is a huge negative as no horse over 10 years old has won since 1927. At the other end of the scale OUR CONOR is only five years old and in 90 runnings only one has prevailed and no horse has won without a prep run for 19 years so that puts a line through THE NEW ONE.

Barry Geraghty travels like a dream and turning for home it looks as if the first time visor has had the desired effect, jumping the last JETZI and myself are both flying and the last thing you want is McCoy on your tail, trust me the last 100 yards were the longest I can remember for a long time. Oi Oi a monster punt personally landed a 9/1 winner poked into the Don and ANDY BELLS punters have also backed him e/w, so all round a blinder. QUEVAGA - she is just an amazing horse and at 10/11 I reinvest courtesy of Corals. Three out I do just wonder if Mr Mullins has been to the well once too often, but wow, brilliant, words are not enough to sum up a fantastic win and what an achievement and in the style she did it in - who's to say there won't be a number seven next year. How unlucky are we not to make it three wins on the trot as SHOTGUN PADDY fluffs the last and is agonisingly beaten a nose into second. We don't trouble the scorers in the last and day 1s punting is very successful and we can all sleep well knowing we are taking a nice little lead into day 2.

The after-racing jovialities began in the wine bar, where I was convinced that we were on the QE2 as The Rock couldn't stand up straight and was swaying around like Shakin' Stevens and this was at 7pm! We decided to get some substance in him and the steaks were nearly as nice as the ginger concierge that has strutted her stuff there for many years. Unfortunately, the steaks didn't have the desired effect as the bouncer of Club 21 reminded us, you two are OK (Pete and myself), but there's no way that one with the red shirt (The Rock Holden) is coming in here. So begrudgingly we hail a cab and head back to our flat.

To be fair to 'The Rock' I think he actually did us a big favour because the next morning we are as fresh as daisies. I say us but I mean Pete and myself. The Rock who is struggling and trying to find something he can keep down from the fridge, tells me that we are to meet fellow Betfan tipster The Greyhound Master, which pleases me because it's a great opportunity to pull the piss out of him. The second day into the Festival, I write:

The Don is on the scoreboard when the favourite bolts up after another masterful ride from King Ruby and our RED SHERLOCK is hampered out of a place.

So first honours to The Don. Our next selection CORRIN WOOD puts in a horror show of jumping for some unknown reason, as he jumped like a stag when winning last time and after hitting numerous fences fades away and is well beaten. Not a great start after such a good winning day 1. In the third KAYLIF ARAMIS is travelling so well and is booked for a certain place when falling three out, which guts me, but not as much as when I realise the winner is The Don's selection at 25/1, now that's going to take some catching. SIRE DE GRUGY looks stunning in the paddock and for all the special sign-ups it's a maximum bet because both of us have made him our selection. Also in the next we both agree on BALTHAZAR

KING and after a foot perfect round of jumping Dicky delivers and once again the sign-ups have had a 6/1 maximum winner.

The Greyhound Master bottles the meet and we all think that he was rather intimidated or just plain frightened of the piss being ripped out of him. The Don ended up smashing me on the second day at Cheltenham and is back with vengeance. Oh, how these results hurt me!

Chapter 11

Bad news at the Cheltenham Festival

On day three of the Cheltenham Festival I'm quite happy with the previous day's winning total of 20 points. That's a decent result but not as good as The Don who racked up more.

It's another spanking day; the sun is shining and the birds are singing, The Rock Holden isn't quite so jovial, although he is in total denial of having a steaming hangover. I know he has by the way his fried breakfast was being pushed around the plate as if it was a roulette wheel. But I can't fault him as he has banged in a 100+ point profit so far this month with his Stableline service.

The racecourse is packed with punters and race fans again as we settle in for the day. I write:

WONDERFUL CHARM runs like most of Nicholls have this week - flat and poor and is never in contention. TOP WOOD runs like the proverbial drain and the day is off to a poor start.

In my opinion, not only because all our money was on DYNASTE, but I think Tom Scu's ride should certainly be up there with ride of the week.

Just what the doctor ordered and we are up and running

with a nice winner. THIRD INTENTION was the Tizzards' father-son combination who was properly smashed up in the betting and we had a great price only for him to hit three out, but we did nick a place in 5th. How unlucky are we not to finish the day with our 2nd winner? That's when CAUSE OF CAUSES is travelling like a dream and the winner, when him and Nina demolishes the last and finishes a very fast and a very unlucky second. Well, another winning day which I am proud of and even more so since that's three winning days on the trot and when you consider the task, I'm very happy with that.

Again we head out with the crowds, drink too much and don't eat enough before rolling back to the flat. The following day Holden tells me that we are to be meeting one of our 'pimps', one of the top three has been granted a pass from Betfan Towers and is winging his way across to have a meet and a beer. Let's hope Big Si isn't too scared to attend. I write:

The only good bit of today was that Simon and his wife Bonnie did show and although the Betfan shares were tumbling at a fair rate of knots as we hit loser after loser, we did manage a laugh and a few wines.

Writing about today with the added advantage of hindsight

is slightly easier because, in short, it was an absolute massacre for all punters. When the winning trainers are in a state of shock, who are there for every moment of their horse's preparation, what chance have we? Since Greedy Friday, which I have now named it, as the Greedy 1s creamed it and the smug bastards killed us all, I have spoken to many tipsters from the top to the bottom of the tree and got very much the same answer "unbelievable results".

Well hands-up, well done Grumbling you beat me fair and square and between us we hit about 13/14 winning bets on the week, which on hindsight is an amazing 50%ish and made all the special sign-ups a cracking 60ish point profit on the four days, at £20 a point that's £1,200 for opening an email. How fickle are a few people? Unbelievably because Friday was crap and a washout, we had people moaning, I know why, I bet the moaners had spunked our profits on other selections and didn't have the brilliant 130 point profit bank we had amassed going into Friday. As I said on my Facebook page, a quote from the greatest jockey, John Francome: "You would have to dig an awfully big hole to earn that."

There really is no pleasing people and it is one of the downside to be professional tipster. However, I was happy with my overall performance at Cheltenham – I had three winning days to the Don's one though he was the overall winner. I hope to be given the chance to take him on again.

I must say though the Festival wasn't the same for me after I received some terrible news - my old, dear friend Ken died in hospital. This really did bring me down and the last two days at Cheltenham were barely enjoyable for me. The passing of Ken has left a huge void in my life as it has many others.

The day after Cheltenham it takes me six hours to return home on the bone rattlers and then on the Birmingham New Street to Peterborough rattler there's no wifi and obviously without Oddschecker, I commit the cardinal sin and copy the Racing Post's price of 7/2 for a tip and post this as a bet. As I get to Peterborough and get wifi, my inbox is full, as most people have smashed up every bookmaker insisting on the 7/2 on what is a 7/4 at best. I have to issue an apology (mainly because the last night at Cheltenham was a very late one). Anyway, all is well since the tip bolts up as expected and a free tip I gave in the Saturday column is only just beaten but nicks us a place at 9/1. I write:

Back to the norm yesterday again with a nice winning day, although I must apologise to my late betting clients as at the moment I can't tip rubbish and could stop a train.

A couple I feel sorry for especially as they joined after the amazing 11 winners on the trot and have had to endure the darker side. I have no worries personally, as I know the strength of my network and it will turn again. Don't forget I have not found the Holy Grail, I am just more fortunate through hard work than most others to have such great trustworthy contacts to back my form and tissues.

Then after a week of fun and excitement at Cheltenham, events catch-up with me and I feel really ill on the Monday. I'm full of cold and my throat feels as if it's stuffed with razor blades. I blame Manchurian Pete, who was coughing and spluttering all week. The next few days are spent playing catch-up and then my attention turns to the potential of the Craven meeting at Newmarket in a month's time. This means that the flat season 'proper' is about to start and while I've had a great jumps season, I really will come into my own on the flat with time spent on the gallops and working up my network of contacts.

Things can't be that bad because on the Tuesday I rack up a 28 points profit and move into fifth place on the tipsters table. Wednesday provides a 12 points winner and everything is looking rosy again as we move into fourth place.

Thursday and Friday are fair but Saturday is a super day with several winners propelling me into the top spot. Indeed, the next week goes in the same vein and then I write:

The flat proper starts at Doncaster on Saturday and today I have been asked to have a look at the race for one of the representatives with a view to backing him in the Lincoln. As always the draw and the going are paramount and as of today the ground looks as if it will be on the good side, but as we know all too well in this country nothing can be taken at face value weatherwise.

Bit of a mixed bag today, we did in fact get a place with MRS JORDAN, who did do what we wanted by leading, but wasn't good enough on the day. I thought BOB KEOWN had won, but he just got mugged after the last fence and came second and although ARTURS OAK was cruising in front and trading at 10/1 ON in running, he couldn't quite last home and also got beaten after the last. So despite all the strong info we have posted a losing day.

I touch base with my mate Steve to see if what I have come up with for the day's Hunter Chase is a winner. Steve is very excited that our thinking is alike and my views confirms his.

Immediately, Steve calls the connections with our thoughts and an hour later confirms to me that it's all systems go. I write:

SILVER TOKEN is the flashy grey horse in question and is

trading with most of the greedy 1s at 4/1. I am on the verge of backing this win only as the fav is a bad one, but I err on the side of caution and back this e/w through my network of bettors and email out the same information to all my clients. The 2 day forecast is suggesting rain at Doncaster, so my advice is to sit on all your bets as CAPTAIN CAT the fav for one will not want any rain at all.

From the off the fav shows why we were so against him, as he doesn't really want to race and sulks in last place, damn, a chance missed of laying an 11/8 fav. SILVER TOKEN is ridden with the upmost of confidence by Tom David and he is travelling so well with a circuit to go he lets him go and the only dangers are in front of him. SILVER TOKEN wins untroubled and never comes off the bridle, the 4/1 looks an amazing price now as he wins totally untroubled. Oi oi that's a nice one stuck up the Greedy 1s. We have hit over 40 points profit on three separate times this month already, only for various reasons to lose them again, now let's hope I can kick on and end an up and down month on a high.

The local Chinese restaurant is calling tonight as the sizzling king prawn dish is the best in the area and the fried battered oysters are to kill for. With the tank full, with no MSG I hasten to add, we finish the meal with a nice bottle of white and sheep's eyes (lychees).

Again, the up and down nature of how I earn a living

comes to the fore and I'm flying once more. I admit to my readers that the past week has been difficult and I write this for my column:

After our Hunter Chaser paying for last night's meal, today is another day, with a very interesting Hunter Chase at Wetherby. With question marks over the front two in the market and three others being blatant non stayers RADHARC NA MARA looks an incredible price at 25/1. Not wishing to get carried away, but if RADHARC NA MARA returns to form he has a great chance of going very close and Holly can certainly ride. I have an e/w bet with some of yesterday's winnings at 25/1 and email out to all my clients and advise taking the over-priced 25/1 on offer with the various Greedy bookmaking firms.

I am catching the train to Doncaster tomorrow and at this moment in time I still have no idea what I am backing in the Spring mile or the Lincoln.

The draw and the going are such vital factors nowadays, even though the clerk of the course will be adamant that there is no draw biases, which we all know is rubbish. I will see how much rain actually falls during the course of the day and also tonight.

I am sure it's our bets and monies which is bringing RADHARC NA MARA into 10/1 from our 25/1 in the betting before the off. Holly settles him near the back and when the favourite makes a mistake and falls she cleverly kicks on and takes 5 lengths out of the field. With a circuit to go I am starting to get animated and very excited as we are going well and with the non-stayers I can see us being second at the very worst.

Three out Holly kicks again and with two slick jumps we win going away. What an absolutely fantastic result - a 25/1 winner, which has won very easily.

We have done it again and totally eclipsed yesterday's great 4/1 winner with a stunning 25/1 winner today. I can say I did tell you that our Hunter Chase form and information is second to none and we still have another 2 months of it to go.

Which fool has been wishing the jumps away in favour of the flat I wonder?

This means I finish March with a strong run; if things have been exciting since the last flat season ended, they are only going to get better this season. I promise the readers of Saturday's Betfan column that I am going to 'kick some proper arse' this year. Will I do it?

Chapter 12

The year-end is near....

So I ended the month with 93 points and third place in the tipster's table but it does take me through the 500 points barrier since joining Betfan.

I did go to Doncaster, a course I really enjoy visiting, and I'm still jubilant about the 25/1 winner previously which means that the flat now has a lot to live up to. I get to Doncaster and find the crowd is not only friendly and jovial but most of them are dressed as if it was a warm June's day! A particularly scantily-clad crew, which had amassed downstairs, in the bar opposite the Ladbrokes station, were already three parts to the wind as the first race was parading and on closer inspection, as you do, its rude not to, The Rock and I could see why.

They had very badly smuggled in bottles of wine which were protruding from the pile of bags in the middle, obviously our stewarding qualities didn't come to the fore as we both happily accepted glasses of the booty. I write in my diary:

Our SILVERY MOON in the spring mile looked great on paddock inspection, where the Don was also lurking, we seemed to be travelling well 2 furlongs out, but as it seemed for the whole day it was difficult to make up ground and the horses at the front during the races came out best.

I didn't have a strong view in the Lincoln and if I had picked ten horses it would not have included the John Ryan winner. The Rock and I spend most of the day in front of the rails bookmakers and the paddock. We did pop back to Ladbrokes and were annoyingly (hehehe) called back to the wine swilling party, who, if possible, were showing even more skin; if all of the garments on show were sewn together there wouldn't have been enough material to cover the Don's bald patch!

The rest of the day was passed upstairs in the owner's and trainer's bar without much incident, although I was told a Newmarket inmate is very well in himself and is expected to win next week and I am allowed to put him out on BETFAN, which is a huge bonus.

After the day's racing ends, The Rock and I head for the Australian Bar in town which is really buzzing as usual and we stay for a couple of hours and decide, while we have still got a brain cell between us to eat.

We head for the China Palace in Silver Street, which on entry is very nice and an indoor fountain is quaint. The meal is very nice and the Chinese beer is OK, but after the third visit to the boy's room, the splashing of the indoor fountain doesn't seem quaint anymore, but a pain in the arse. The rest of the night passes without incident and we head back to the hotel. The following day, I write:

I am awoken by an extremely excited Irishman, on the mobile phone and not in my bed, I hasten to add, who is extremely bullish about the O'Brien trained BRACELET, who runs in Leopardstown today. He tells me in no uncertain terms this will win, so I quickly gather myself and back it at 9/2 and send out my email advising my clients to do likewise, win only.

I'm also told that LEO LUNA will run a big race at Ascot and ROYAL MARSKELL, who I have tissued up at 7/1 will go well at Doncaster. I am amazed when I spot we can get 14/1 with the Tote on ROYAL MARKELL and LEO LUNA is a more realistic 11/2. I advise backing these two e/w singularly and also with BRACELET putting the three in an e/w Trixie.

The track is much more sedate and reserved today, but I suppose it is Mother's Day and all our best friends are being treated to their lunches; my brother is doing the good deed today and it's my turn the next day.

BRACELET bolts in at an absolutely amazing SP of 7/1, with hindsight I so wish I had put her up for the Oaks, which she has now been cut to 8/1 for.

With LEO LUNA deemed a non-runner, the pressure is firmly on ROYAL MARSKELL to at least place, if he cops it we have won over 250 points in a day. Wow, that really would be something to crow about! ROYAL MARSKELL is travelling like a dream at the 2 furlong pole and my heart is pounding as we are looking like having a 7/1, a 14/1 and a non-runner in our Trixie but no it doesn't happen. He fades out of contention and we have to settle for a 50 point winning day, never mind!

Reflecting on the long train journey home is always unavoidable and I am gutted to be so close again, but hey, if I was told I would multiply all of our stakes by over 50 times that morning before leaving for the racecourse, I would have been over the moon. Well a fantastic winning day, but if only! The next day I'm still gutted about the result and I write:

It was a great winning day for us yesterday, which has put us third in the table with over 80 points profit and my goal of over 100 points again doesn't seem a million miles away now.

My Irish connection who gave us BRACELET yesterday is again ringing and I am immediately thinking he has had his praise and ra-ra's yesterday. He has been told that the ex-owners of the Ted Walsh inmate NEVER NEVER, who has just been sold to the McCain team, will win today. This is trading at even money and after yesterday I'm thinking we should stick with a man in form, so I back this heavily personally and email out for my clients to do likewise. The very shrewd Amos stable are going for a touch on HOT WHISKEY and the word is the 13/2 will disappear as quickly as a bride's nighty, so we all back this e/w as well.

I hope we can continue our good start to the week as Friday is Ken's funeral and I am not looking forward to it one bit and I just don't know how it will affect me and in this game as you all know, you have to be 100% totally focused.

The bride's nighty and the 13/2 on HOT WHISKEY are things of memory as he goes off at 3/1 and is always well up there and finishes a good second, so a small win. NEVER NEVER from what little I could see through the Hexham mist is headed 2 out, but battles back to win going away and also best odds guaranteed comes up trumps again as we get 6/4 SP.

Another super winning day to round off a very up and down month and this should take us over the 90 points profit, but we fall just short on the 100.

I try to settle down to find the winners but again the cards are quiet, as is usual with a big festival around the corner. I do however get decent information and the members of my late service top the leader board at the beginning of

April after some decent priced winners.

With the end of the jumps season approaching it means it's the Aintree Festival - a hugely important event in the racing calendar and one of the few races to actually reach out to people who aren't normally interested in horse racing. I tell my members:

The start of the Aintree festival today and it's already looking like being a busy one for us.

Early doors we back both NAKUTI at Lingfield, where Silvester Kirk has made an eye catching booking of Ryan Moore and we have a very rare MAXIMUM on HUSTLE BUSTLE at Evens, at Wolverhampton in the 5.45. I also put these two in a win double. I also email out in the Fox Hunters at Aintree BRUNSWICK GOLD e/w at 28/1 and HARRY FLASHMAN e/w at 100/1.

This is the first Aintree meeting I have missed for eight years, as I have my great and not only racing friend's funeral tomorrow. At this moment in time I am not sure whether we will be betting, but I'll see how I feel and will play it by ear.

Is Ryan Moore at fault over NAKUTI's defeat, or is it my pocket talking? After watching it three more times I'm not convinced either way, whatever the verdict the best horse didn't win.

BRUNSWICK GOLD wants a head start in the Fox Hunters and dispatches with Stuart Robinson and as it nears the high street I am praying he is pulled out as I have had some good e/w bets on him.

HARRY FLASHMANS big white face is prominent, but as I've said don't expect him to win, but he could nick us a place, he travels well for a circuit at a well backed 50/1 and the excitement comes to nothing as he fades away, but credit to him he does finish. THE LATE BETTING INFORMATION sit tight as their CLARET CLOAK finishes third at 4/1 backed into 7/2.

To finish off our day we have a facile win on HUSTLE BUSTLE as he leads from start to finish and wins by an easy 3-4 lengths. It's not quite happening for the ANDY BELL's clients at the moment as the loss by a head on NAKUTI has cost us 40ish points. I feel confident and it's just a matter of time before we start climbing the BETFAN table.

In all, a frustrating day as we have landed a maximum bet and we have not managed to kick on through a contentious ride.

So the next day is Ken Lindsay's funeral. RIP great man.

As Winston Churchill said: "Good and great are seldom in the same man."

This is what I wrote about the following day's funeral for my members:

The church for Ken's funeral was at capacity, with standing room only. After a very nice church service we retired to The Lenwade House for drinks and eats, which was also packed. It was nice to catch up with a few of the now retired jockeys like Alan McKay, Joey Brown, Gary Bardwell just to mention a few. John Ryan was still on a high after his amazing Lincoln win and Geoff Huffer was still drinking away the proceeds of Cockney Rebels achievements.

Both John Walk, ex-Ipswich, and Robert Fleck, ex-Norwich, still looked as young as ever. Even the jockeys' agents found time and made a show, Paul and Gareth. After far too many wines and hugs, the flock starts to disperse and we also bid our farewells and head for home.

Because of Ken's funeral and my potential reaction to it, I have still managed to do my homework and write the columns for the following days. I write:

PINEAU DE RE first 6 places is my Grand National free tip at 28/1, I know the Doctor's stable have all backed this and are confident of a huge run.

I feel like crap this morning and with all my work complete the only remedy is a livener. I head into town and meet up with Tony the Machine and quickly neck a couple. I head across the road and have a cash top up on PINEAU, but Corals the meanest of bookies are only offering 25/1, as I have asked my bettors to get me on earlier in the week and they are all full up, I have to accept the 25/1 and have another decent e/w bet.

My mobile is red hot this morning as everyone wants a National tip, numbers I don't even recognise are calling and numerous shouts across the street. I could easily look a right chump if this goes tits up, don't people realise this is probably the hardest race of the year to get right?

It does sicken me that the people are queuing onto the street to get their bets on in Corals and are being mugged off by being given a lesser price and its half of my drinking pals or ex pals later, from Weatherspoon's responsible.

Tony and I shoot a few games of pool in the Bear to kill some time as I am getting very nervous and twitchy by now. We decide to get closer to home to watch the big 'un, maybe a big contributing factor to this decision is I've marked so many peoples' cards that a public flogging may be called for.

We arrive at the Tuns pre-race and by now the reality of how much I have tendered on the race is beginning to hit home, the beer isn't helping either. Luckily enough I have arrived too late and all the National bets in the pub have already been laid and I am able to slip under the radar.

Obviously, you have all seen the race so no need to talk you through it, but when Leighton Aspel is close up two out, I can't hold my emotions in anymore and start screaming at the flat screen, after

4 miles PINEAU DE RE is apparently still swinging off the bridle and puts in another great jump at the last to win nice and cosily by 5 lengths. As they pass the post, Leighton is certainly cooler than I am, as the Tuns has just had a whirlwind hit it. As all the pub's losing tickets are hitting the floor, my twenties are hitting the bar for bubbly all round. After the lucky seven bottles, well so I am told, I am dancing on the tables and surely being a right pain. 6pm and Cabbage arrives and is about four levels below us on the booze stakes. After being refused any more drinks in the Tuns we stagger across the road to the Swan, where we get the same result, no more drinks, thank goodness for Tony the Machine as he takes the lead and sorts me a lift home.

The following day as I wake, my mobile phone is paramount and I can't find it. After an agonising hour, it's hidden with my monies on top of the cupboard, I don't know why, but every time I'm drunk I hide my monies. I am desperate to check what texts I sent out with what monies I have bet on them and making sure they have all been confirmed. All is cool, as all my bets were placed and confirmed. It is nice reading the 51 texts of thanks I have and with all the people I have told in Weatherspoon's and also ALL YOU 50,000 on my free tip and of course mine and the families, I wonder how much I have taken out of the betting industry, £1 million????

I love this life when things go this well, I really do.

Chapter 13

The stress of tipping for clients

As a professional tipster it would be nice to bow out and soak in the glory of a fantastic winner. Saturday's National winner is a case in point - an unbelievable result in one of the world's most famous races but despite having a huge hangover the following day, I still had to punt out advice to my subscribers.

Fortunately, the contact that delivered the National winner was on the phone with another great tip running at Fairyhouse. He is like a dog with two tails as he got onto the Dr Newland winner early in the week and really did clean-up and today he offers another great priced winner.

After this it's back to the books and, as part of my regular research, I tissue up a decent horse called Sealous Scout at 5/2 and can't believe he is trading at 5/1. I put in a call to my contact who knows the Donald McCain set-up and my thoughts are confirmed and the horse is a brilliant each way bet at 5/1. I then put this out to my members as a decent tip and also offer another one that has come from a contact.

Later on, I also get a tip for a horse that is priced at 13/2 for the late information betting service and then decide to go out. Here's what I write:

A trip today to our small local independent bookmakers and then to Corals to pick up my Saturday's winnings. Without being rude, I do hope I don't meet any of the people I put onto PINEAU on Saturday and get dragged into Weatherspoon's as I really don't want any alcohol today. As I enter the local bookies I get thanked for ruining his big day of the year as it had somehow got round the whole town and nearly everybody had backed it. Good, I'm thinking, up yours - if you weren't so greedy you could have laid it off at over 36/1 on Betfair, but I do keep my thoughts firmly to myself, as he is not a happy chappy.

Luckily the trip to Corals goes without incident and I collect and sneak out, without being accosted or dragged into the boozer. I've mentioned before that putting a bet on in Corals, and indeed all of the major bookmakers, is becoming increasingly difficult for me but having a good payday such as this really does put a spring in my step.

On this day, I have a cracking 5/1 each way tip which wins a good race though my other choice runs poorly. The late betting service also scores with its 13/2 winner. I write:

All my clients prospered yesterday, with a really good winning day.

We have loads of information coming through this morning and I have got to decipher how, what and where, we are going to place and bet them.

CALCULATED RISK, in what looks a very short price of 2/1 in a big field, comes through very strongly ridden by Ryan Moore. On looking at the race in detail, as it often is, there is a lot of dead wood and, in my opinion, over half the field can't win.

In a smaller field, LIBACCIO is being touted out as he has been working really well at home and is expected to make a winning reappearance at 15/8.

Finally, the recently moved HARMOODY at 9/4, who is having his first run for Joseph Tuite after leaving Dandy Nichols, is going to be ridden up with the pace and kick for home coming round the bend; that is the plan anyway.

My email advises backing all three win only and also an e/w trixie.

Not wishing the LATE BETTING SERVICE to feel left out at midday I get the Donald McCain trained GO CONQUER. For all you form buffs amongst us, his form figures are a quite amusing. F.U. McCoy is booked to ride and as the information is coming very strong for this stable at the moment, I personally have a good bet on this at 9/4 and advise via email all my clients do likewise.

Anyway, Ryan Moore's judgement isn't at its best on CALCULATED RISK as at the 2 furlong post he is still 20ish lengths off the lead and then entering the final furlong he absolutely flies and is only beaten by a fast diminishing three lengths.

The LIBACCIO field has cut up to only three runners and Paddy Power, who I advised the bet with, are still showing first 2 places. I call them and the Girl confirms this is the case, although I do find it extremely hard to believe, but who am I to say? LIBACCIO is a shade disappointing in my opinion and is beaten by the outsider of the field into second. So if Miss Paddy Power has got her facts correct and not just reading off the screen, our e/w trixie is still in play.

HARMOODY does exactly what's on the tin and is running on in second and kicks off the bend to win nice and cosily at a very well backed 15/8.

So, on the singles we just about break even with a 1st, 2nd and a 3rd, with the jury still out regarding the e/w trixie.

The form figures of F.U. doesn't stop GO CONQUER leading all the way and bagging another winner for the LATE BETTING SERVICE at a very well backed 10/11 making our 9/4 look a steal.

So, all in all, a very satisfactory day's work.

With only ten days gone in April, I've made 60 points in profit and the late service isn't far behind. Again, I'm focussed and working hard at finding winners, hammering contacts for information and reading up all I can on what is happening with trainers and jockeys. I write:

It's very quiet this morning at the moment, but we have got the heads-up for John Gosden's at Kempton tonight. TARTHAAB has apparently been working with winners in the mornings and is very well fancied to run away with his race tonight. 5/4 is on the short side but I decide to email this out and back it myself.

I am on the verge of putting up a no bet day to the LATE clients, when I spot that Marco Botti has a 20/1 shot running in the first at Kempton, BRYON GALA. He has been placed on all but one of his starts, been a short priced favourite on three different occasions, of his seven starts, which denotes to me that he has been showing ability at home, has a good draw and a well capable 5lb claimer on board. I mention all of this in my email and, as I have not been told anything, we have a relatively small e/w bet on him at 20/1.

It's time to have a look at the Scottish National runners for Saturday and see if we can get an unprecedented double-up after our 28/1 winner last week. I think we have found one for the Scottish National, but I just need to make a couple of phone calls to hopefully confirm my thoughts.

BRYON GALA is first to run and what a race he runs, only beaten by the favourite and finishes 2nd, what a feather in one's cap that would have been if we had have copped. But, then again, our great racing game is a marvellous leveller and TARTHAAB runs like a ponce and comes 4th of 4. Piss poor.

However, THE LATE BETTING SERVICE continues to amass the points and firms up its place in the top three of the table, with four winning days on the trot, while ANDY BELLS clients are up and down like a bride's knickers, but they can stick it, as we have amazingly passed the 500 points profit barrier this month in less than a year with BETFAN, at just £20 a point that's a cool £10k earned tax free in 10ish months.

Another relatively quiet day, but I do put up a 20/1 and a 9/2 both e/w and chance a very small e/w double. I am waiting for the nod on one at Wolverhampton tonight, which if it materialises I will pop it on to the LATE BETTING SERVICE.

My thoughts are in fact confirmed for the Scottish National and we will be having a good punt, but sorry folks no freebie tomorrow as it's going on my main ANDY BELL service.

We don't get a look in today, but hey at 20/1 and 9/2 we can afford a few misses, it's not like backing even money shots, when you have to get two out of three to profit and we know that is impossible long term. Also our Wolverhampton bet doesn't materialise, so nothing to add or bring to the party.

So there you have it, I was brought on board at Betfan as one of the country's leading tipsters and in less than a year, in just over 10 months in fact, I've racked up more than 500 points in profits. In real terms, that's £5,000 tax-free for every £10 a point bet. Or, as many followers will be doing, for anyone punting £100 a point that's £50,000 tax-free for doing nothing except open an email I send out every day.

And then again, there are still people griping about the results, about the odds that I get but ultimately I can't please everyone all of the time and most punters cannot deliver winners as regularly and as often as I do. I don't let the naysayers get to me and I'm focused on delivering even more profits and better results for my growing membership services. Though that's easier said than done!

After the Scottish National, I write:

The Doctor was king for us last week, when his PINEAU DE RE won the National, with our free Saturday tip and another Doctor was our nemesis yesterday, as the Doctor Koukash owned GRABIEL'S KAKA beat this week's free Saturday tip BROWNSIE BRINK whom we had backed at 10/1 e/w, although we did make a small profit on the bet.

It was the same case when our COURT MINSTRAL at 17/2 jumped the last and had the beating of the short-priced favourite MY TENT OR YOURS, only to be mugged by the Cheltenham buzz horse COCKNEY SPARROW. Once again a small profit, but this Saturday was certainly not what the Doctor ordered, although we made a small profit on the day.

KINGMAN was scintillating and well deserves to be head of the 2,000 Guineas market at 2/1, after a very easy win and more importantly clocking a two second quicker time than the Fred Darling winner.

We couldn't get the English and Scottish national double as our MENDIP EXPRESS was pulled up.

Though we did it again on the LATE BETTING SERVICE as we made it five winning days on the trot, when Choc loomed up on my advised MILES TO MEMPHIS and won nicely at 3/1. In all a very satisfactory day's work, as I personally won a right nice few quid again and with all my ANDY BELL clients winning a small amount and THE LATE BETTING SERVICE clients clearing up again multiplying their preferred stakes by 24 times.

Today, I can see that THE LATE BETTING service clients have jumped into second on the BETFAN top 10 table with 92 points profit and long may it continue. Fear not the ANDY BELL mob as we will be there, as we always are come the time of reckoning on the 30th.

I must say that I find it quite unusual, if not intriguing, that I run two services with essentially the same search criteria and the same network of contacts but here we have the late service doing substantially better than the usual Andy Bell service. I'm at a loss to explain why this should be and say so to my readers. Even the upcoming flat season, with the start of the excellent two-day Craven meeting, cannot cheer me up and I'm increasingly keen to find some big price winners for my service. Indeed, some critics may say it becomes a little desperate because I break the rules on day one and email some advice out later than I am expected to normally. That's because I got a nice piece of information on a small each way priced horse that did quite well.

Then we are at the Craven. Simon 'The Rock' Holden has travelled down to stay with me and this is what I write:

Whoop whoop, the day of reckoning is finally here; the start of the two day Craven meeting and boy does ANDY BELL's service need to shape-up, because after all my mouthing, there's going to be nowhere to hide come Thursday evening.

On our way to breakfast, I get a call telling me that when King Kieran got off TRUE STORY after its last piece of work, he was adamant that he is a Derby horse.

On hearing this I steam in and get all my bettors to grab me the 3/1 which is on offer for some lumpy amounts and also email out the same message.

The breakfast is good and The Rock is now rearing to go,

but I just have to pop across the road to the Swan and just smooth things over after my last antics, so I am told, pre our National win. Luckily the owner, Robin, is in there and greets me with, 'Andy you were a naughty boy last time you were in here, dancing on the tables and as for drinking the whole of Mr Hart's bottle of wine down in one and then filling it up with water, while he was at the little boys room was very funny, but not nice' - all, luckily, said with a smile and a chuckle.

Ex-school teacher, Mr Hart who is a member of three Highclere syndicates will see the funny side, eventually, I hope.

MUNJAZ is expected to win the race after TRUE STORY, but at the moment this is no rocket science as Mr Gosden could win with the yard cat, at 13/8 I also email this out as a cracking bet.

We pick up Mr Jolly and arrive at The Rowley in plenty of time and get a prime seat in the owners' and trainers' bar overlooking the paddock and also spotting the flimsy day one attire.

As all our bets are done and we have a driver, the Grolsch is able to freely flow and things are warming up nicely. Then when The Don waddles in, I can't help thinking that he is carrying a lot of condition and would certainly come on for the run. He joins us at the table, without visiting the bar, I hasten to add. When Simon asks him if he has bought a pie shop, he doesn't really cotton on, but when I ask him if he has won any of his pie eating contests, the penny drops and he was up and puffing away. Poor old Don.

Our local boys are downstairs and on a pub jolly and

wanting their cards marked, so hopefully I can come up trumps for them. I give them all TRUE STORY and a string of decent bets (£100 x 2, £160, £140, a £620 and various others) are winging their way to the rails, OMG I think, I have double that on, but theirs create more pressure.

At the 2f post I am thinking TRUE STORY is under pressure as the very well backed, into favourite, Irish horse under Spencer's guidance is swinging away, but as soon as we hit the rising ground SDS gets a proper response and the further he goes the better and wins by a pulling-up 7 lengths. Oi Oi Bellie Boy's hit the Newmarket turf running and has bagged our first winner.

Downstairs is now carnage and the line of drinks that welcome me is quite frightening, I am sure I can cope though, it's the kisses and cuddles which are more worrying.

We don't have long to wait as MUNJAZ runs in the next and as expected he looks stunning in the parade ring with his coat shining like silk in the bright sunshine.

The bus load of raging Bungay boys are now rampant and ALL pile in again on MUNJAZ.

MUNJAZ is placed nicely on the outside and when asked at the furlong post, there is only one winner and we have two out of two at Newmarket and won all my clients nearly 30 points profit. The two winners have the Bungay bus paid for and all the entrance fees sorted, the kitty is full and the evening meal is sorted, so good luck wherever the boys pitch up later, but I can smile and be proud as I have done my bit.

Pity I only ever opened the Cheltenham page and it pains me to write about it, so I'm not, but we win 18 points on the day and that's a great start to a great meeting.

With pockets full of cash and accounts fully topped up, we stop at the Swan on the way home, there are no antics this time and immediately I start on the red wine, after I don't know how many, but we are both very well oiled by the time we say our goodbyes and head for home, with another big day in the offering tomorrow.

There are two things to say about handing out free tips to friends and acquaintances - firstly it makes me look great and reinforces my position as one of the UK's leading tipsters but, crikey, it also opens me up to some abuse should the tips not perform.

I'm always pleased to help a punter, especially those who don't get to attend races very often to enjoy the spectacle and thrills of live racing. I love the lifestyle and there's no doubt on days like these I get a lot of envious comments. I don't mind....

Then there's day two of the Craven - a superb meeting. I write:

Phew! A great start yesterday and that eases the pressure

for today; don't get me wrong, that's not the job done, but a great start. Yesterday I was told that BELLE FILLE of David Brown's is expected to run a big race in the opener today and when I get it confirmed this morning I have no hesitation in putting her up as an e/w bet and advising on taking the 20/1 on show.

ALJAMAAHEER is 13/8 which looks on the shortish side, but he has the class to win this easily.

Last, but certainly not least, Jane Chapple-Hyam thinks MULL OF KILLOUGH can win this race for the second consecutive year and at 9/2 he looks a cracking e/w bet to nothing, with the eye-catching booking of Adam Kirby.

All my bets are now complete and emailed out, so we can take the leisurely drive to Newmarket for day two of the Craven meeting. As soon as we arrive I know that the choice of shirt is the wrong one as it is totally different weather and quite cold and windy.

The owners' and trainers' bar isn't cold whatsoever so Simon and I pitch up in there. It seems busier today inside and outside.

We want to record our BETFAN TV slot from the track, but we can't find a good enough filming point, without shoving Nick Luck out of the way. As always, it is manyana and we settle down for a fantastic day's racing.

Another BETFAN power joins us, Chris, who is starting a new service soon to complement his existing one. We are unable to hold him in the trainers' bar for long, as him and his World War 2 binoculars soon disappear to his beloved paddock.

BELLE FILLE plays up in the stalls which isn't ideal, but breaks well and is always up there. She does stumble slightly and loses her action as she hits the rising ground at the 2 furlong pole and is very frustratingly beaten less than a length back in fifth. This little filly will be winning races, unfortunately not today when we had our monies down at the 20s.

I think Paul Hanagan needs to join the now portly Don in the gym, for a different reason, as his rides don't seem to be filled with power packed finishes, rather tame and weak and his ride on ALJAMAAHEER is shocking, losing by less than a length after being caught well out of his ground and flying at the finish. He should have won by at least two lengths.

MULL OF KILLOUGH is expertly placed by Adam Kirby and when he kicks for home a furlong and a half out he flies three clear, only for a boys in blue chaser to appear and close, thankfully Adam has nicked the race and wins nicely and finishes off the second day on a high. The Rock and I walk out of Newmarket after the two day Craven meeting, with me knowing I have now had two good winning days on the trot and making a long awaited recovery, with over 27 points profit at the Craven.

It's straight home tonight as we have a couple of nice bottles of red waiting and I'm cooking two steaks weighing in at just under 2 kilos.

Chapter 14

Bank Holiday racing really does test me...

As I have said before I love horse racing and support all sorts of causes and want more people to enjoy the events. I accept there's a lot more for people to do nowadays and, for some, the sport is losing some of its appeal. That's a shame but then it's getting harder for owners to spend so much money with such poor prize money on offer and the racing calendar is often, shall we say, perplexing.

For instance, I'm not entirely sold on racing on Good Friday. Not for religious reasons but because the racing powers-that-be have created a card of big prize money racing which, I believe, should be shared out more equally in the racing calendar. I could drone on about how racing can be improved and made more attractive and the lack of mainstream TV coverage is a real setback. The BBC dropping coverage will also hurt in the long term and the coverage on Channel 4 sometimes borders on a student broadcasting project. (Why are they using long range lenses in a strong wind - you can't see what is happening!).

My work as a tipster progresses well - by the 18th the late service smashes through the 100 point barrier. Though I'm still harsh on myself and I write:

If I hadn't of been such a knob when mistakenly putting up OBSERVATIONAL at Newmarket as a WIN bet only at 14/1, when getting beaten by a nose, we would by now had eight winning days on the trot. I take a little solace from the fact that my clients know my style of betting and hopefully they bit the bullet and thought 'What's that prick on?' and taken it upon themselves to back OBSERVATIONAL e/w at the advised 14s.

Further to my thoughts about racing on Good Friday, I don't like the racing on any Bank Holiday, to be honest. One reason being that there's so much of it on I find it very difficult to concentrate and get my teeth into it. Also, I question the planning aspects as in the east of England where we have Fakenham, Huntingdon, Market Rasen and Great Yarmouth, which in itself is crazy, because all they are doing is diluting their attendances. But then I'm not in charge. Anyway, back to Yarmouth and I write:

First day of the two day meet at Yarmouth and with so much racing, I just concentrate on three meetings: Gt Yarmouth, Fakenham and Huntingdon. It's going to be difficult at Yarmouth today not seeing Ken's smiling and jovial face around the place and I bet the Guinness sales are down as well.

All my bets done and emailed out then I pick up my father and Mr Jolly and we head for the coast. It's quite busy and on entering the owners' and trainers' bar, I think it's a nice touch that a pint of Guinness is up the corner with Ken's funeral programme. I am also part of sorting a permanent picture of him in there.

We back two losers and thankfully the local lad, Louis Steward rides a cool race on PIAZON and can be called the winner two out, which lessens the blow. Whilst there I get a call saying that the Nick Skelton stable really fancies WOOD BANK at Huntingdon. I can see he is trading at 13/8 and taking on an odds-on favourite, which doesn't perturb me as the information I get from this stable is brilliant. I bet this on Betfair and email out on my mobile advising the late service clients do likewise.

I have a meeting with one of my/our very important tipsters/advisors set up for this afternoon and I am very encouraged and excited by what he is telling me with regards to what we will be betting during the course of the flat season. He has already given us two MAXIMUM bets and two winners. I am told we have another for the weekend and also one for Friday at Sandown, which surprised me and should be a good price.

THE LATE BETTING SERVICE does it again as WOOD BANK does exactly as I am told and leads all the way and bolts up by 7 uncontested lengths, with the odds-on favourite never in contention.

That should bang us over the 100 points profit for the

month again.

Although some of the lads are going out in the town tonight I don't fancy it and head for home, like a good boy.

One of the more enjoyable aspects of being a professional tipster is that you have to regularly take note of up-and-coming horses and then watch their development as they progress into sure fire winners. Things become a tad more difficult when following quality horses for the really prestigious races but it's a worthwhile task to undertake because snapping up ante post prices can be a profitable job. This also means that those wanting to do so must appreciate what to look for and how they can compile their odds on any particular horse.

I pride myself on my ability to tissue up a decent runner and this talent really comes the fore when we need to find a winner for the Oaks, the Derby or even the 2,000 Guineas. As the flat season slowly progresses, some horses do catch my eye and I not only make a note of them but I flag up their potential to my readers. For instance, I write:

I open the Racing Post, after a very near and "if only" day yesterday, as both my FREE tips came agonisingly close, to find AUSTRALIA and SHIFTING POWER were trading at both ends of the spectrum in the betting as AUSTRALIA traded at 4/1 second fav and Frankie's mount was basically the rag at 100/1. Coming into the dip, I have to check the colours as Frankie is just about leading the stands side group at 100/1, KINGSMAN kicks on as they hit the rising ground and looks the winner, but "King Kieran" has other ideas as he comes to take it up and drifts markedly across the course and nearly collides with our very fast finishing AUSTRALIA and wins a shade costly. Leaving our 100/1 shot SHIFTING POWER a gut wrenching fourth.

Although to the eye AUSTRALIA looks a super candidate for the English Derby, I do question the 7/4 on offer and I certainly wouldn't be in a rush to take it and our 100/1 fourth SHIFTING POWER heads for the French equivalent.

This morning, as I said in my 7am email, I find it astonishing that the MIGHTY YAR is trading at a huge price of 13/2, it's not often I can say this about the Greedy 1s, but according to my tissues, I think we have found one that has slipped through the net, as I have punted this big myself, I advise my clients to do likewise and snap up the VC super price.

Just after the 1,000 Guineas, I get a very exciting text, reading "Our very special filly TAGHROODA, who's homework suggests she is the best 3yo filly we have, is fully expected to win the 5.00 here today and win it well, on her way to the Oaks."

I pass this message onto the LATE BETTING SERVICE clients and on the back of this text I then have my biggest bet of the weekend at evens on her. I also take the view, that if my contact, who is the bollocks, thinks this much of her and I am willing to back her win only today at evens, we should also have a swing at her for the Oaks at 10/1 e/w, which I do and also advise.

OMG she certainly possesses class in abundance as TAGHROODA scoots away from the field and wins by an eased down 6 lengths. The LATE BETTING SERVICE clients have not only secured a maximum winning bet today, but are all now sitting on 10/1 ante post vouchers for the Oaks on a 3/1 shot.

A good winning day personally and also for both my services.

Everyone made a decent profit over the two days and we are all on TAGROODA at 10/1, who is now as short as 5/2 in places, for the Oaks. I then have awful mobile phone problems which show how reliant I have become on the technology. It scuppers me for a few days but there's Chester on the horizon - a track I really like but I no longer go there. I explain to my readers:

It's been a relatively quiet week as I do not bother to attend Chester anymore. I have had eight years on the trot drinking and abusing my body within the walled city. Graham, an ex-publican, used to be my roomy and by god that's a man that could drink for

England. One particular night stands out as we were staggering around looking for our next port of call, for what seemed like ages, when suddenly he said, 'Let's try this place.' On entering I didn't notice anything out of the ordinary, but when he said 'Oh, let's try upstairs' I did wonder how he knew. Anyway on arriving upstairs it was full of scantily clad beauties and a roulette table. Let's try roulette, he says innocently. After buying our chips and I had my first win, a scantily clad beauty approached me and said, 'Two more wins and you'll be OK'. Not knowing what she meant, I continued. Now wanting the little boy's room I asked Graham where it was, his quick reply was up the stairs turn left, first on the right. 'How did you know that?' I enquire and with a smile the perv confessed he had been here before. Back to the roulette table again and my lucky 23 came up and this time the scantily left me in no doubt what my chips would pay for behind the curtain. I will leave it to your imaginations whether I accepted or declined like a good boy.

I love the Classics, I think they are greatest sporting attraction in the country - they have fun, skills and thrills as some of the world's finest horse flesh try to make an impact on the toughest and most famous races anywhere. The jumps season is also coming to a close and I write:

It's the last day of the jumps season proper and we were all in on the Doctor's horse ARDKILLY WITNESS at 10/1 e/w in the BET365 Gold Cup. The stable were once again going for a touch on this relatively lightly raced eight year old, with the only question mark over the extended distance. I had also heard encouraging reports about the James Franshaw trained, Hayley Turner ridden SPIRIT RAISER, who caused a stewards inquiry before the race had even began, as I emailed him through at 10.15am at 33/1 and by the time my clients received it at 10.19 he was 14/1. I expect Sportingbet took a whole fiver on him and ran for cover like rats. I also make SPIRIT RAISER my free e/w bet in my column.

Column sent, bets done, stewards' inquiry sorted with the admin dept and a couple of hours until the off. Ipswich lose in the early Sky match, so that's a good start to the day, as we couldn't stomach them passing us by coming up if unbearably we (Norwich) go down. Norwich has a nice easy run in with Man Utd later today, who will be the hardest test, as they will play like men possessed for their new manager, then Chelsea who seem to be more interested in Europe than about the league anymore and Arsenal, with fourth place secured will only want to lift the FA Cup.

The LATE BETTING clients who are sitting on a right good profit this month of over 100 points get their first email of the day, advising them to take the 11/8 available on ARAB SPRINGS at Donny tonight, I have been told this is a right good machine and whatever it does tonight it needs to be entered in ALL notebooks NOW. (You heard it first here).

As I said on my BETFAN TV interview, most bookmakers are a joke now, as the huge betting race of the day approaches, the BET365 Gold Cup, of the top seven in the betting SIX are shortening and then I am asked why I don't bet on the rails anymore. This is why: I have got 10/1 best odds guaranteed on a now 8/1 shot and first 5 places.

ARDKILLY WITNESS jumps and travels into the race like a dream and I am thinking the good Doctor has done it for us again, but turning for home the warning signs are there and, unfortunately for a non-stayer, we fade tamely away out of contention.

If Hayley Turner had of been any softer on SPIRIT RAISER it would be laying on her hearth in front of the fire tonight! Talk about a racecourse education, walked out of the stalls, sauntered into midfield and gracefully bounded, with no assistance from the saddle into fourth. Get them notebooks out again boys and girls and write SPIRIT DANCER in big red letters under ARAB SPRINGS, as a schooling in public.

As I am licking my wounds and counting my loses, I get a call saying that the Burke team thinks they can beat the Stoute hotpot COSSETED with TRIXIE MALONE in the race after our bet ARAB SPRINGS. As I have had the Stoute information for the day in the previous race, I have a good bet on this at 11/4 and email out the LATE BETTING service.

ARAB SPRINGS wins like the good horse I was told it was and if it's not already in your notebooks please enter it now. I have now radically cut my day's losses and I am amazingly waiting for TRIXIE MALONE to turn personally, my losing day into a winning one.

The very game TRIXIE gets the biggest cheer of the day as she leads all the way and keeps sticking her neck out all the way to the line. I have now turned my day completely round as I am now sitting on a profit. The LATE BETTING service has incredibly done it again making over 25 points profit on the day with two bets, two winners, as the poor old ANDY BELL clients are sitting on a loss. All I can honestly say is that ANDY BELL is only having a blip as his long term record shows, but maybe it's an idea to be part of both ANDY BELL and THE LATE BETTING as they are completely devoid of each other and offer totally different and individual services.

Sunday morning is nice and peaceful with not a great deal showing up on the form or the tissues. Not a great day's racing unless you are French, Italian, Irish or Chinese, oh and although we try to, let's not forget the Germans, as we only have Ayr and an aw meeting at Kempton.

Chapter 15

Answering the critics

The coming days don't get any better for my service but the Late Service is flying. I head to London for a great meeting with an owner who owns a large string of quality racehorses and who, thankfully for us, loves to have a gamble. I write:

I have a meeting in London today, so I catch the 8.47 to hopefully strengthen my contacts for the coming flat season. I have a very early call whist on the rattler telling me that Dandy Nichols will have a winner at Wolverhampton. COME ON DAVE is in the 2.20 and is ridden by his son, I am told that the even money is a good price as the plan is to jump out and make all, so I email this out as a MAXIMUM bet.

COME ON DAVE is backed into odds-on, so once again we beat the market and does jump out and is four lengths clear after the furlong and stays at least that in front for the whole race. A nice maximum bet landed, but that doesn't detract from the worst month ever ANDY BELL is enduring.

Whilst on the train home, I am advised that the Henry Candy's owners are all going to Windsor and are fully expecting COSSETTE to win. Getting the internet on a train now is virtually impossible, the amount of questions that have to be answered is incredible, it's easier to get a mortgage at the moment. I think sod this and call Smudger, who's always at the computer to look at Oddschecker. 5/2 seems a fair price and I put this Windsor evening runner up on the flying LATE BETTING SERVICE, which is fortunately propping up the ANDY BELL service and clients who are in both.

*After a row with the taxi driver who wants to charge me an extortionate £2 a mile, which is twice as much as the London black cabs and will equal my return train ticket. He can go f**k himself and I get out halfway and bung him £15 and tell him to like or lump it. I don't mind paying but I hate to be ripped off.*

Luckily our row had escalated within walking distance of an independent bookmakers and the Swan pub. I enter the bookmaker's to a frown and told to forget any bets that I may want, I tell him that I only want to watch COME ON DAVE and tell him to back him and lay it in running if he wishes as it will lead. After DAVE bolts in, I think maybe I have gained a few brownie points, but I'm sure the town's 25/1 national winner is still fresh in his mind.

Yes, you guessed the Swan is now the next port of call and just as I'm entering my second bottle of wine and getting into the swing of things, Gitty, my lift arrives to drag me home.

COSSETTE is travelling well under a very still and quiet sitting Dane O'Neil and wins very easily by four lengths at 5/2. A good day for both services ANDY BELL has backed a maximum and once again the LATE SERVICE has bagged another.

The next few days carry on in the same vein and I'm becoming despondent that I can't find winners for both services. I write:

Thank goodness April has finished, well that's probably selfish of me to say that, just because ANDY BELL has had a terrible month, I mustn't forget that the LATE BETTING SERVICE clients who have had a cracker, WINNING and making over 163 points profit, with an amazing 102% ROI and an incredible 59% (better than 1 in 2) strike rate.

This morning I am meeting Owen "the fixer" aka BETOWEN for breakfast at the local greasy spoon. During my poached eggs and his monster fry up we discuss Newmarket, funny that, he mentions that he is waiting to see if a race is split as he has a real nice plot bet Saturday. Don't worry I will sneak it on my ANDY BELL Saturday email. We decide to meet every Thursday from now on to keep each other up to date now the flat is in full swing.

The Punchestown festival is in full swing and we back a 12/1 shot e/w with no returns, but in all honesty the cards look impossible today. Golly Gosh the LATE boys and girls also have a loser, so no drawings today.

Then things pick up (as I always knew they would) and I start having decent priced winners again. I write:

A good start to the month for ANDY BELL and thank goodness for that and it was nearly so much better: a 5/1 winner and unfortunately our 6/4 shot couldn't quite carry the 12lb extra to victory and get us a good win double and 40ish points profit.

Today is huge for me as I love the Guineas weekend and from today onwards the flat season really starts and there is so much to be learned for the rest of the season from this two day meet.

This year's 2000 Guineas looks as competitive as I can remember for a while and if one of five horses won you wouldn't be overly surprised. The ground adds another complication as KINGMAN and KINGSTON HILL both seem to need a bit of cut, AUSTRALIA reportedly the best that has been through Coolmore, will hopefully not fluff the start and run his race. TOORMORE pricked his ears when winning at Newmarket's Craven meeting and looks to hold some back for himself.

Anyway, I'm full of verve again with the winners coming once more. I've mentioned before that having a poor spell always brings pressure and with a paid service to support those wanting my advice are right to be critical. They are spending money for my insight, skills and contacts and they are right to criticise me when things don't work out. I'll publish what I wrote at the time. This next section is over a few days but underlines what can be happening in the background.

With my colours firmly attached to LOVING SPIRIT in the Victoria cup, as the immense confidence was portrayed to me in no uncertain terms, I had my biggest bet of the flat season on him e/w at 16/1 and 14/1 so far. All connected and close just could not contemplate him being out of the first 5 and were expecting much better. He had been trained with this race in mind all pre-season and this was meant to be his day in the sun and a nice touch for a small stable.

I put him up as a maximum e/w bet to all my ANDY BELL members and also wore my heart on my sleeve as I put him up as my free column bet.

The form figures were not impressive on my next selection, GREEN WIZARD at Haydock, well pretty dismal in fact, but Steve confirms he has had immense schooling in the last few weeks and if able to keep on his feet will go very well.

Finally the clever Don Cantallon has AS I AM running also at Haydock and if the young apprentice can get his fractions right, as he will lead, he is also expected to go close at 16/1, if it's not too soft.

On such a busy Saturday the late service has two bets that come through, the Clive Cox trained HASSLE and John Gosden's GATEWOOD e/w at 13/2.

GATEWOOD under a good ride from Frankie starts off our busy day brilliantly as he wins well at a very well backed 4/1 making all our 13/2 look a steal. Better to come as HASSLE also wins at 9/4 and gives the LATE BETTING SERVICE a super Saturday and making 49 points.

LOVING SPIRIT absolutely bombs out and with no apparent excuses, unless the ground had gone too soft after a pre-race downpour. GREEN WIZARDS schooling has in fact helped as he jumps a good confidence boosting clear round and nicks us a 7/1 place.

AS I AM is pulled out as the ground is deemed too soft, so another day awaits him.

Today we back ABSOLUTE SHAMBLES and the lightly raced, John Fergusson trained MEMORBILLIA and also put them in an e/w double.

GEOFFREY CHAUCER is the selection I put up on the LATE BETTING SERVICE as I am told this is now the number two Derby hope behind AUSTRALIA.

Not a good day at the office as both my e/w selections are the aggravating fourth and GEOFFREY CHAUCER should have won, but had no room at all and finished a very unlucky third.

I arrive at the airport to fly home this morning, after a week in Malta with my father and Pauline, I haven't mentioned it before, because I got a few snide remarks from punters that were under the impression that they are solely paying for my holidays, they were and are in a very small sense, I agree, but surely correct me if I'm wrong, with over 400 points profit for the ANDY BELL clients in less than a subscription year, at just a pony a point (£25) that's a cool 10 grand tax free and, I hasten to add, THE LATE BETTING service has contributed another 250ish points profit (£25) - that's another 7.5 grand in less than six months!

I can assure you that I bet all my selections and a pony a point is far below my average stake, for all my clients that makes it SEVENTEEN AND A HALF GRAND and more for me personally, so surely I'm paying for your holidays and you don't hear me complaining; I'm genuinely happy for everyone. Of course, if for the very small majority, the real reason is that one has spunked it on one's own selections and are in a BAD mood and dare not tell the WHOLE TRUTH AND NOTHING BUT THE TRUTH to the wife or partner then obviously poor old Andy Bell is the fall guy and has to take the brunt, which I fully understand and can go along with, as in my younger days I have done that and been there.

Enough of that, all I want for all of my clients, and

people who know me closely will agree, is that I'm happiest when everyone is winning and enjoying their spoils.

You see, I do listen and I'm acutely aware of how things are when we aren't winning. Anyway, I had a nice break in Malta and after unpacking my holiday clothes, it's time to pack again for the great racing event that is the Dante in York. A great festival, well organised with some fantastic northern trainers and owners all keen to outdo each other. If you only ever get the chance to go to one meet then head to York but be aware that the nightlife afterwards is mad - this is a pub-goer's town that really does know how to party.

Chapter 16

It's York and back to winning again

The Dante and a trip to York. I had a decent winner the previous evening which is a nice confidence booster with such a busy week ahead. I do all of my homework before setting off at lunchtime for the famous city with the aim of arriving at teatime to enable me to book into an apartment, unpack and perhaps freshen up. I have also prepared my notebooks and information sources for the following morning - I like to get ahead of myself! However, I am concerned about the going as I don't trust the going reports in the least. That means that I will have to walk the course myself early the next day and I can gauge the going by how far the high heels I have borrowed from Simon Holden sink in. This is what I told my members:

Nothing to back during the day, but Hunter Steve has two big bets lined up for us tonight both at Southwell. POPAWAY in the 6.00 and later on the Newmarket trained BROUGHTONS WARRIOR. I decide to back POPAWAY singularly and then double it with BROUGHTONS WARRIOR. As I shouldn't and very seldom do, I also put up BROUGHTONS WARRIOR on the LATE BETTING SERVICE as in all the eyes of who's who this is too good to miss.

POPAWAY kicks our evening betting off wonderfully as he wins oh so easily. I meet Simon 'The Rock' Holden in the revamped Living Room and settle in to have a couple of quiet beers until he suggests that we go down the cocktail route as it is 'two-for-one'. I am not overly impressed but allow him to twist my arm. Race time and BROUGHTONS is always very well placed, until he gets pushed back into 5th on the home turn, my heart sinks as personally as I have had a right swing at this and also a real nice double pending. He soon recovers and wins with consummate ease. Between my two services we have netted over 60 points profit and had a right touch which does not bode well for my quiet first night.

We have a table booked at the famous The Waterfront restaurant with the even more famous chef and owner Richard. He greets us from the steaming kitchen door as we enter and he duly informs us that he has hardly any food in and in his famous Yorkshire accent moans that he is tired. The Dante hasn't even started and Richard's cupboards are bare and he is ready for bed.

He convinces me that his Tomahawk steaks are good, which I must confess are not top of my ordering list or even knowing list. The Rock has his T-bone and we have a bottle of Chablis. Next time I hope he doesn't give me the handle of the Tomahawk but he does do me sauté potatoes and by now is quite jovial. A bull's blood is the next choice of libation and things are boiling very nicely. The Rock doesn't let me forget about my super winning evening as Blondie slips the bill on the table. We bid our farewells to Richard, who is shouting about 'Smarties Moviesta tomorrow', no chance in this soft ground I think. Look out York tomorrow as I feel in form after two cracking winning days.

First day of the usually very informative Dante meeting and thankfully the weather is shaping up nicely. A very funny start as I walk through the gates, Simon 'The Rock' Holden is profusely sweating and I suggest he joins the always red-faced Jim Goldie under the horse water spray cooler, then he tries to bullshit me into believing that it is sun block. As I attempt to enter the trainers' bar I am told I have to wear a tie, so I don't bother and head for the champagne area where, yes, you have to wear a tie. I can't remember this from my many previous visits. A bit snookered now so I get directions to buy one, the best choice is a stripy one which clashes a tad with my stripy shirt. With my now traffic light look, which matches The Rock's very pink sun lotion head.

I have had a huge word for MADAM CHIANG in the Musidora stakes, the Simcock team have told me this is their Oaks filly and at 10/1 I advise my ANDY BELL clients to get on e/w.

At 25/1 the front running STORM KING looks too big a price for his relatively new trainer, so I also include this in my selections and suggest a small e/w double on the two to kick off day 1.

All my bets placed and The Rock appears supporting a

silver bucket and some bubbles, never wishing to disappoint, I gratefully accept.

As the Grumbling Don passes in his long overcoat, can you believe that, he mutters some choice words in our general direction and disappears. The lawns are covered with lots of white skin which is slowing turning pinkish, The Rock did kindly offer to rub his sun lotion forehead on a blonde's legs for her, she smiled and declined his kind offer.

STORM KING does lead as we thought he would, but at a suicidal pace and ultimately pays the penalty and fades away to the rear.

King Kieran is always travelling very sweetly on MADAM CHIANG and as soon as he sees daylight he powers through and wins nicely and in doing so nets us a lovely 10/1 winner and sets us up with a great winning day on day 1.

After the race, it is confirmed that she will take her chance in the Oaks if the going is softish. I don't think she is good enough to trouble our LATE BETTING SERVICE clients ante post bet at 10/1 on TAGROODA, which is now 5/2.

The ice bucket is replenished and amazingly a steaming Grumbling Don appears awash in sweat, as Penny is not to be seen, I wonder if he has been using his World War 2 binoculars to look more in the lawn direction than the course. He steams up to the bar and amazingly reappears with a........... bottle??? No way Pedro, a glass to share our champagne, he is priceless, but we do have to laugh.

My tie is now hanging around and looks much better around a brunette's neck than it ever could around mine. The Rock and The Don are having an in depth discussion about, I don't know - it can't be fashion, maybe binoculars or overcoats, who cares, I leave them to it.

First day of York and I walk out head held high as I know I have nailed it with a 10/1 winner and made all my clients money and can have a drink knowing that we have now had three winning days on the trot. No Richard as he is booked up tonight and the Living Room is the first port of call. The Rock's face is now redder than ever as his get pissed-quick-cocktail-plan falls flat on its face, as he boldly orders us all one and, hehehehe, on race days it's not two for one and he has copped a £70 round. Excellent!

As we have a major day's work tomorrow and the BETFAN Tower boys are coming, the rest of the evening passes without incident and the only thing that accompanies me home is the trusty kebab.

Looking back it's hard to believe that I am so restrained in a town that likes to enjoy itself. Anyway, I continue to regale my followers about day two at the Dante:

With my tie knotted securely, not tight enough many say,

the Rock and I leave my apartment and head for our meeting with the Tower boys.

We arrive at the course and head towards the County bar as that is where they have pitched up. We meet Simon, one of the three Tower boys, Eddie the Stat and Harry Potter, who has been let out of his chamber for the day. After five pints of gut and bladder busting pints, we finally convince them that the flesh clad lawns and champagne bar is a better option. As we all know, Champagne, no food and sun is a mix for disaster as many are already finding out and also the two of our party are beginning to flag.

ANDY BELL's selections are MISTER UNIVERSE who has been burning up the Mark Johnson gallops, the big priced MR SNOOZY at 14/1 and the Newmarket runner COMPTON BIRD also at a juicy 12/1. I back these all singularly and also put the juicy priced MR SNOOZY and COMPTON in an e/w double.

After unfortunately having to break the 'seal', I am surprised that all four are smoking Big Mac-style cheroots. Eddie the Stat is the first one to turn green and admit defeat by jumping on his, Harry Potter is puffing away like Ivor the Engine and waving it about like his magic wand and Simon's eyes are watering like they did last night when he realised the cocktails weren't two for one. On closer inspection The Tower boy, Simon's, is a fake as he gave up smoking it after giving them out; that's just not cricket Simon.

MISTER UNIVERSE looks like winning at the furlong post only to get run out of it late on and finishes second to give us a small profit. As COMPTON BIRD has been declared a non-runner at Newmarket, our hopes for our e/w double and e/w bet are now pinned solely on our 14/1 shot MR SNOOZY. From his poor draw MR SNOOZY runs a gallant race and gets us a place to land our e/w bet and also our e/w double.

I bid the four remaining swillers goodbye and arrange to meet them later. As I am walking slightly waywardly I can smile to myself at another successful day's work and making another day's profit for us all, which is now four on the trot.

I managed to get back to the apartment with the intention of freshening up and checking out some information for tomorrow's runners at Newmarket but unfortunately I fall asleep. A few hours later I awake and it's turned 8pm and there are 23 missed phone calls on my mobile from the members of our party. After a quick shower I turn up at the designated place only to find that the Rock has left in a moody because the other three have stood him up to catch the train home. Despite my best efforts, I couldn't get the Rock to return so end up having a drink with a famous trainer who tells me about a great horse they have running at Hamilton the next evening. Because I really do have to get up early the next day, I decide to have a quiet one and return home for a good night's sleep. This can be a very stressful and tiring job!

Chapter 17

Forget the nightlife

I know it looks like I spend most of time either in the bookies, the pub or on the racecourse but that is 'working' for me. However, no matter what happens on the night, I have to be up bright and early the next morning poring over the form. This happens after the York meeting because I'm heading to Newmarket, early doors. I write:

Up nice and early as I want to get my form and the cards mostly completed before my three hour drive to Newmarket. I check out the chances of DIVINE and decide if what I was told about his homework he is a must e/w bet at 4/1. Also get your notebooks out as my one to follow, ARAB SPRINGS runs in the second. Although it's a stronger race, I am convinced it is good enough to secure his third win on the trot and I also bet and email this out. Finally BIG BAZ at Newmarket and the SDS ridden MAMBO PARADISE.

On arriving at the very sparsely covered Newmarket car park, I wonder if it was the right decision to leave York. Ryan Moore gets our day off to the best possible start as him and ARAB SPRINGS wins well and virtually ensures our fifth winning day on the trot. I am standing with William Muir pre BIG BAZ race and he is very disappointed with the outcome as I am and thinks a return to the aw or softer conditions are in order. SDS misses the break and never looks like winning the 5f sprint.

It was a good day's work all told in Newmarket, I have five winning days on the trot and things went well on DIVINE.

I also hear that 'Eddie the Stat' spent his holiday on crutches, as we got the lightweight so drunk at the York meeting, he fell over and ended up in plaster. I wonder if he tripped over his pencil or dropped his pencil sharpener on his toe. I hear there is no room to sign the plaster cast as he has filled it full of his life dependent stats and figures! I maintain the belt and holiday test are still the best guides: if the belt keeps getting loosened and you're enjoying lots of holidays, there's no formula or hours of needless work required, it's easy, you are winning.

All joking aside, I'm obviously not the only professional tipster working in the UK. Some might say that I'm not the best (though the statistics will prove that I am among the very best) and the stress of running a service extends to all of us. One of the sad truths is that we all have winning streaks and losing runs – it is part of the game and the trick is to have more of the former than the latter. Easier said than done! But it's also right that members vote with their feet if they aren't getting the returns they are paying for. I explain this to my members:

Today is bright and sunny and we have no excuses regarding the ground at the moment; if any of your preferred tipsters are not performing and making you money at the moment or in the next few weeks, I think you need to be looking at your personal portfolios and other services within the BETFAN network, as it's going to be an awful struggle for them come September-ish onwards when the form books are once again turned upside down.

I did mention that I didn't see Penny at York with The Don and when he started talking about Northern pro's in his Sunday column, I did wonder for a moment where this was going but, true to form, he only meant the trainers.

After emailing out my selections, I get ready for the Sunday lunch trip out.

We decide on the Hoxne Swan, which used to be one of my old haunts and the trouble I used to get into there was mind-blowing. We once put so many chairs on the huge open fire it set light to the chimney. The landlady once found her husband shagging one of the barmaids in the loos and the next thing we saw was the barmaid come whizzing past the bar window, as she had jumped out from an upstairs window onto the road, only to hurt her pride heheheh. Jim's bike was also tampered with on many occasions, but the best one was when we tied it up and hung it from the chandeliers. Fellow drinker Simon who had a habit of sneaking off half-way through the night in an attempt to escape the pokey dice box, so we cured that by removing his shoes at 9pm-ish. During an unsavoury brawl between us and the Eye boys, the now deceased Teddy Garnham at the ripe old age of 80, clambered off his chair so he could clock one of them with it, only to miss and hit our own Paul Potter. I was not the most popular punter they had when I rode Alec Jolly's horse through the pub and packed restaurant.

Good job it is a sleepy little village, as one morning I awoke to go to work and my car was still running with the driver's door wide open and the lights on. My mother was worried about my state one night as I had passed out in the outside toilet blocking the door and attempted to wake me with the yard broom by prodding me through the window and when that was unsuccessful she had the bright idea of throwing water through the window to awaken me, when that didn't wake me she was than panic stricken that I was not only going to be outside all night, but was now soaking wet. After a cold night in the privy, I finally awoke to a find I had a black eye. Shit, what had I done? I had no recollection of my previous night's exploits and after a sheepish couple of days, Mum realised and told me it was her broom antics. Luckily, as a few say, I survived to tell the story. Those were the days.

JERSEY BULL kicks our Sunday's betting off in the best possible way, as he does in fact lead all the way at 11/2 as expected and wins very easily despite young Willie dropping his whip a furlong out.

My information seems spot on as NEW STREET is smashed up in the betting and as the gates open it's showing at 7/2 making our 13/2 look a steal. Unfortunately, we have found a sleeper as both are five lengths clear of the third and we are beaten into second, so a small profit.

In all a very satisfactory day's betting as we have made 14 points profit and made up for yesterday's small loss.

The ensuing days are just as successful, I have a seven-day winning streak though I'm tempted by some good information on the all-weather tracks. I really do dislike AW tracks and avoid them wherever possible. As usual, I begin a regular jaunt to the gallops in Newmarket to have a look at some of the great horses there. I write:

Only a brilliant ride by AP McCoy denied us a 20 point profit yesterday, oh such small margins between winning and losing!

Bank Holiday Monday and I am heading up to Leicester racecourse in order to smash into the William Haggis trained WONDERSTRUCK, as I have been told she has really flourished since her debut and if her very shrewd trainer's lofty entries are anything to go by, this Ribblesdale charge must win well today.

I am also putting WONDERSTRUCK up as a MAXIMUM bet to all my Betfan clients, coupled with the Karl Burke trained TRIXIE MALONE, who won well for us last time out and I am sticking with this gutsy little front runner again today here at Leicester and MAMBO SPIRIT looks a bet to nothing each way. With all my emails done, I can now finish my last leg of the nearly 3 hour journey.

We have a slight stewards inquiry as I enter the car park as what must be a Chelsea pensioner posing as a steward, questions my jockey's car park badge, it is real by the way, just the badge's owner isn't sitting beside me today. Anyway a smile and a very sharp intake, no, now I am lying - a very very very sharp intake of breath and we are through.

I am disappointed that the fish stall has been replaced by a clothes and racing book stall, but I do buy a Mick Fitzgerald's autobiography, Better Than Sex, and also an old John Francome one, to add to my ever-growing collection.

TRIXIE MALONE runs her race and attempts to lead all the way but the handicapper has now caught up with her and she finishes a gallant second. As we thought MAMBO SPIRIT is an e/w bet to nothing and gets us a place. We are just hitting the cross bar at the moment, not far away, but not close enough.

It is now raining quite considerably here and quite miserable, which is made worse by the fact I am told it's sunny and lovely back home. My day doesn't improve as Mr Haggis now considers the ground unsuitable for WONDERSTRUCK and pulls his filly out, which is much better than her not acting on it and doing my dough. She goes to Newmarket on Friday to contest the maiden, which also has the long awaited racecourse appearance of the £3.7 million purchase HYDROGEN.

On a strict line of form through today's run away victor the John Gosden trained winner REWAAYA, today's maximum bet WONDERSTRUCK, who beat it by three lengths last time must have had an excellent chance, Mmmmm a chance of a maximum missed, we will never know for sure.

A billy no mates' night is looming for me as most sensible people are enjoying the sunny Bank Holiday with their BBQ's flaming and a few tinnies at home, so I was gleefully told. The closest I will get to flame grill tonight, will most probably be a Tandoori Chicken dish from the Taj Mahal in Northfield Street.

The first port of call is The Highcross, which is a Weatherspoon's run establishment on the High Street. Far from being the first in there, a few look as if they have camped here for the whole Bank Holiday, I am certainly on a different level and have got some catching up to do. After a couple of pints of the good old £2 a pint Stella, I head past the train station and into the city centre and into The Long Bar, where is Simon Holden when you need him, as this is a very stylish cocktail bar and we all now know how he enjoys buying them at the moment. Not in a cocktail mood tonight, so bottles of Stella for me. A tap on the shoulder and it's one of my adversaries, who had been standing at Leicester today, who will remain anonymous. The sob stories don't get any better, as he tells me the on-course markets are dead and there is no money left in the ring. When I pose the question: is it their own faults for being so greedy, not offering concessions, always a point or two behind Betfair and sometimes ten and twenty points behind on outsiders? That might be the real reason, once again it falls on deaf ears. Or maybe they had it so good for so long now it's a reality check and they now need to enter the 21st century as there is so much information available at our finger tips that all of the mug punters are skint and gone.

Anyway, the beer he has bought me tastes good, it's a bit of company and an easy wind-up. We go our separate ways after a few, believing that both our opinions are correct.

I surprise myself as the glitzy lights of The Real China restaurant entices me in and I must say I am very pleased as it was lovely, so is the waitress and also the added bonus of no toilet roll in the fridge needed tonight, as no Delhi Bellie to fear for tomorrow's journey homewards.

Chapter 18

I'm proud of anyone who tips

As I mentioned previously, adding to the strain of finding winners for paying members is the competition from other tipsters. It's a strange world because I'm always happy to see a service do really well and then I'm gutted that it isn't me knocking the winners in. Indeed, I write:

What's this new service that has 'appeared' at the top of the BETFAN tree from nowhere? I have been working my butt off all year, as has the rest of the BETFAN tipsters I'm sure, to amass what now seems like a poultry 500 points in a year, only to wake up and see THE SHREWD TIPSTER suddenly appears with over 1,400 long term points profit. He may well be very good and only time will tell, but it does feel like a kick in the bollocks. Enough moaning and stress or Lord Howie (another Betfan tipster) may well be attending my funeral.

Anyway, I am leaving this morning and heading to Huntingdon with a rare hope that the rain WILL arrive. The forecast sounds promising as it predicts 15mm of rain, which is ideal for our bet in the first.

I stop at McDonald's on the A6 to put my selections up and decide as I know our easy Sunday winner NEVEROWNUP doesn't want rain and will not run if it does arrive. With this in mind I email out the mud lover KING HELISIO ridden by A P McCoy and an e/w steal JACK LUEY, who runs at Redcar at 4/1.

I arrive at Huntingdon and to my dismay they have missed all the rain and I have gone against our very easy Sunday winner NEVEROWNUP in the hope that the forecasted 15mm would arrive.

The rest is history as they say NEVEROWNUP bolts in and our bet in the first never happens, at least JACK LUEY nicks us a place

When I started my service with Betfan my aim was to rack up more than 100 points of betting profit every month. An ambitious target and I have done very well. Again, I have a slight blip in producing the goods which means a dip in profits. It's nearly the end of the month which means I don't have a lot of time to recover the drop. More stress!

I send out a tip which turns out to be an absolute pig before the race and a major problem to load. Pity the stalls handlers who did such a great job to force her in, as she came out last and stayed there for the whole race. Not a good start to the day and then my next tip wins in very cheeky fashion. On Facebook one of my happy punters messages me and I reply: 'From chump to champ in 30 minutes!' I picked up 20 points on the day. The next day I write:

We have some marvellous racing at Sandown tonight, why ever isn't this a Friday day card? I shall not suggest a Saturday as it's already overloaded and a nightmare.

I have two very strong early messages this morning, both at Sandown, Sir Michael Stoute's trained ABSELL and the Richard Hannon Jnr trained TIGGY WIGGY. I email both these out early and suggest a big win bet on each and also a win double.

The Rock Holden was on his soap box this morning in his column, with a scathing attack on Haydock's clerk of the course, Mr Tellwright, regarding his going descriptions. I am pleased that somebody else has jumped on the band wagon because I have been banging on about this despicable behaviour for years. As we all know, the ground can beat any horse. I just wonder if his poor analysis of the going was in conjunction with the massive Scoop 6 pot, maybe Freddy boy wanted it to continue another week or two and wanted another spoke put in the works, or maybe there was nothing sinister at all, just Michael Fish's training of Mr Tellwright.

As I comment in my next email, I am not going to be like some tipsters and sit on my laurels and have no bet days and cut my points tendered just because I'm over the magical 100 points profit barrier for this month, I am going to continue piling in.

I am told that ANSAAB is a tremendous e/w bet at 8/1, the

drop back in distance is supposedly meant to suit CHILL FACTOR and my final bet is the 18/1 shot WHIPLASH WILLEY e/w. I am well aware that we have a lot of money/points laid out today and wonder whether I should have hidden behind my profits a little bit, only time will tell - 'fortune favours the brave'.

I now have two days planned racing at Newmarket, it's the opening meeting of the year on the July course. It's just a mile or so up the hill from the Rowley Mile course.

Our first runner of the afternoon is ANSAAB, he has been well backed from our 8/1 into 5/1 second fav. A furlong out I think we may just win, but he never quite picks up and finishes a clear third and makes us a small profit on our place money, as we expected. CHILL FACTOR is shite, enough said I think, roll on this evening.

TIGGY WIGGY carries all our monies as ABSELL has been declared a non-runner and scuppered any chance of landing our double. In what, on paper, looks a tricky little event, the Scott Dixon 'Cock Of The North' has been really well backed into favouritism and a couple of others are quietly fancied. If TIGGY is going to represent the Hannons at Royal Ascot he must reproduce what I have been told is sparkling homework on the track tonight. As soon as Hughsey makes his move a furlong out, the result is never in doubt has he flies away to a four length victory. All roads now lead to the Royal meeting than possibly on to the Super Sprint at Newbury.

I am disappointed/pissed off whatever you want to call it, when I check how many points I have put up on my last runner of the day, WHIPLASH WILLEY at 18/1, only to see that knobhead Bellie has mistakenly put him up win only, surely my punters know me well enough now and have noticed this little #### up and backed him e/w, I'm sure?

Anyway, although I can't take any credit for it WILLIE runs on very strongly into third for a place. As Delboy so rightly says, 'HE WHO DARES WINS', we have made 22 points profit and that's allowing for my faux pas, so another super winning day.

So there you have it - so much stress that I make a schoolboy error when sending out advice. As I say, I have a good rapport with my members and most of them, surely, would realise that I'm sometimes a clown when opting for wins or e/w bets. At 18/1 I'm hoping that common sense would have won the day! Anyway, it was another cracking month which saw me rack up 125 points in profit. Let me spell that out - that's £1,250 earned for not doing a lot but open an email and spend £10 a point! To really cheer me up, the Late Service has also had a great month too.

So we enter the back straight of my first year as a Betfan tipster; will I come out of the final turn in front? Will I suffer an incomprehensible set-back and pull up? Only time will tell. The flat season is in full swing and I'm working with a network of great contacts. I write:

This morning I have information and tips coming out of my ears, so hopefully we can piece the jigsaw together and get June off to a good start.

At face value, I have a ludicrous double, which I am emailing out today, I think MUBTAGHAA and MANDERLEY are certain winners, I know there's no certainty in racing, apart from the GMTs crap jibes every week, but these two are as close as I've seen for a while and at the suggested prices, the double pays even money. Also, I have two front runners, which are both expected to go very close, DUBARA REEF at 10/1 and BY RIGHTS at 14/1 and finally the excellent Doctor Newland's HAWDYERWHEESHT at 11/2, who has been schooling very well at home, to email out, all as e/w bets.

We are not out wining and dining today, as I have three acres of grass to cut before next week's forecast bad weather and I may even give the chickens a treat with fresh straw! I know I have to get all my jobs done today, as I have a big day booked out with the boys tomorrow.

HAWDYERWHEESHT ensures that our day starts of well as he secures us a place as we thought he would and a small profit.

The first leg of our double MUBTAGHAA, from the all-

conquering William Haggis stable wins as expected for us and sets up our day. DUBARA REEF, who I knew would lead, but not at a million miles an hour and our fate is soon sealed as he fades away very tamely. BY RIGHTS our 14/1 shot also comes out like a bullet, but the difference this time is he stays there and lands us a fantastic 14/1 winner and a great punt. All of a sudden the skies are blue and the grass is green again and whatever happens to our double, we have hit June running and are having a fantastic day.

Surely the standout form of the Guineas fourth can't spoil our day under Hughsey? She certainly doesn't and MANDERLEY wins very easily under a super confident ride from the man, job done, a 14/1 winner, an even money double landed and a certain e/w bet copped, so in summary a Super Sunday.

Chapter 19

Super Sunday – another day passes into legend

It really was a 'Super Sunday' since I racked up 36 points in profit - or £360 at £10 a point! That's a good day's work in anyone's book. The next day begins with some mixed results, for instance getting beaten by a neck while watching the race in Corals really isn't a good start to the day, but I'm out for a good time. I write:

The beer is flowing in the Bear and Bells and my pool is top notch, as I kick The Machine's arse and ease a nice £60 out of him at £10 a game. I think the landlady has her eye on the Machine, she would eat him for breakfast and spit him out in little pieces, that's my opinion anyway. We wander up the street to Weatherspoon's and I start drinking spritzers to The Machine's dismay, because when this happens things always seem to go tits up, somehow. I hold a score bet for Tony on CANT CHANGE IT and I watch it bolt in on my iPad at 3/1, so that is all my pool hustling profits gone in one fell swoop. Luckily for me the next three all lose so I am now £80 up on the day. That's only lent as it will be over the bar by the end of the session, even in Weatherspoon's.

Thankfully, before things have gone too far, I get a very strong message for JUPITER at 15/8 in the 9.00 at Windsor, which I put up on the LATE BETTING SERVICE. I get the Machine to put me a cash bet on this in Corals, across the road and also Tom to back it at Galleons in Guernsey.

It's now nearing tea time and we are unable to get a cab for an hour, so we have the mad idea of jumping on a bus, as by car we are only fifteen minutes away from our next port of call The Swan. After twenty minutes into the journey, stopping at villages even I have never heard of, we are further away than when we started and by now I am absolutely dying for the little boy's room. It's funny how at this precise moment, discarded coffee cups and bottles all of a sudden seem to be my main focal point. Thankfully, I do manage to last out as we finally arrive at The Swan and I make a bolt for the loo, thank god for all day opening, Arhhh, phew and not even a damp patch to put under the hand dryer and as Mick Fitz said in his autobiography, 'It feels better than sex'.

The next day sees me the worst for work, for as the youngsters of today would say, 'I am hanging like a bastard'. My spirits are improved when I discover that JUPITER has bolted up by eight lengths - a race I missed because I was already asleep/passed out. Unfortunately, no one can see the state I am in and my mobile is busy with calls and texts. With some tips given I prepare to leave home for Yarmouth where I am meeting King Kieran to sign some photos of himself on KRIS KIN and NOTHERN LIGHT for an auction, as my daughter has had the mad idea of shaving all her hair off in aid of a blind children's charity. Not mad to do something for charity of course, but surely she could have, I don't know, jumped out of an aeroplane, or I would sponsor her to go shopping for a new wardrobe of clothes for Simon Holden. Anyway, I spoil the mood by watching my big tip get beat by a neck despite looking like a 16/1 winner. I write:

I knew that Yarmouth would be quiet tonight and the sparseness of the car park confirms this. All the pictures are signed and safely tucked away in the car and we can start work. I meet The Colonel aka Kevin Minter in the press room and we have a chat, he could be a good face to bring to the BETFAN table in the future and we go through the card. One thing Yarmouth deserves good praise for is its sandwiches and the soup in the Press room, which are, as always, spot on.

Mr Haggis wins the first with his ADAAY. I join the biggest queue of the night and thankfully it's not to have a bet with the Greedy 1s, as I want value for my money, so it's the fish stall and I have a lovely Cromer crab and a plate of whelks.

Our GENIUS BOY that we backed last week wins very nicely tonight as does our final bet, the very green WISTAR at 5/2 once again making our 9/2 look great, under a very good ride from Buick. I can't bear to walk the streets of Yarmouth tonight looking for some amusement, as there will more life in the Don's vest, so homewards James it is.

So I had a great winning day at Yarmouth and picked up some great information. I also spend some time this week going through the cards for Epsom. As I've said before, the weather can be crucial for the big races so I check the forecast and then make my selections based on soft going. This change of ground means that some of the ante-post favourites aren't looking so good so I hope to pick up a few well-priced winners in their place. Over the coming days my work pays off and I rack up some great priced winners - two at 14/1 in three days! Not even a week into June and both of my services have delivered 90 points in profit.

I've also been talked into taking on the Grumbling Don in something of a grudge match. I'm not a fan and we have digs at each other in our Betfan columns. Anyway, there's a change in the weather forecast which means I have to change my plan of attack slightly and opt for the horses that prefer 'good' ground. This grudge match also means there's a bit of a juggling act required, as I have to tip in every race in my quest to beat the Grumbler and attempt to put what I think are my best and strongest tips to my loyal clients. I write:

After much deliberation and hours of painstaking study and, of course, numerous phone calls, I finally submit what I hope are my SUPER SEVEN tips to BETFAN. From these seven, my ANDY BELLs clients' bets are GRAPHIC, who is trading at 7/2 and is trained by William Haggis. In the 3.20, I split my stakes between VAINGLORY at 11/1 and the Ed Dunlop trained RED AVENGER at 25/1, both e/w and I can't believe that the front running ALMARGO is trading at a huge e/w price of 8/1, as he had valid excuses for his last two defeats and finally we sneak a hottie in under the radar from Goodwood, STEPPING OUT, win only at 5/2.

With everything complete, I now have an hour before racing and the battle commences.

RACE 1. The Don's e/w bet on AMULET can't get his required lead and fades away, Marmite Spencer totally cocks up what could have been a dream start for me on JUST THE JUDGE as he can't get a run and finishes full of running in 3rd.

RACE 2. SENNOCKIAN STAR is the 11/1 e/w selection of the Don and has far from the perfect build-up as he has to be reshod before the start and finishes unplaced. My SOVIET ROCK which we have bet at 6/1 e/w, sets a suicidal pace and pays for it in the final furlong and also finishes unplaced.

RACE 3. In what on paper looks like a two horse race, the Don selects GREGORIAN and me GRAPHIC, which I also select as one of my better ones and have emailed this out to my clients. GRAPHIC runs 2nd and is beaten by a vastly improved FRENCH

NAVY.

RACE 4. Both the Don and I select VAINGLORY as an e/w bet at 11/1. This is also one of the two selections to my clients, as I also add RED AVENGER, e/w at 25/1. Both The Don and I lose with VAINGLORY, but RED AVENGER very unluckily in my opinion is bulked back into third, ANDY BELLs clients have had a nice 25/1 place, but in our personal battle we are still to trouble the scorers.

RACE 5. The Oaks. The Don sticks with his Irish Oaks 10/1 winner, MARVELLOUS and I also stick with PALACE from the same ownership, who to me looked as if she needed further. Also a month ago I have put up an ante-post bet up on TAGROODHA at 10/1 with my LATE BETTING SERVICE. Both MARVELLOUS and PALACE unfortunately fight out 7th and 8th, BUT oh yes BUT, TAGROODHA wins with ease and the LATE boys and girls have copped a right nice anti-post winner.

RACE 6. We both agree that the very progressive THIS IS THE SPIRIT is the one to be with and thankfully the scorer can wake up and put some scores on the boards.

RACE 7. In the lucky last NOVA CHAMP from the very shrewd Stuart Williams stable is The Don's 28/1 e/w selection and my final selection is the Mark Johnson trained front runner ALMARGO, who I really fancy big time, so much so, I put up him up as a win only bet at 6/1 and I have also put him on my private service at 8/1 e/w. SDS gives ALMARGO a brilliant front running ride and wins going away with ease at an incredible winning price of 7/1.

Phew, I have tipped the last two winners in my Grumbling Don challenge and have finished a very difficult looking day with a nice profit for my followers.

THE LATE BETTING service has had a fantastic ante-post winner at 10/1 and made just under 40 points profit.

If that's not enough, our under the radar 'HOTTIE' STEPPING OUT, at Goodwood grabs the rail and wins with a bit in hand at 5/2 for ANDY BELLs clients.

With the DON v ANDY BELL challenge points, ANDY BELLs personal clients and the LATE BETTING service, we must have nearly amassed nearly 100 points PROFIT on the day.

An absolutely amazing WINNING day ALL ROUND and I think I have earned and I am going to have a few pints of ice cold Stella.

On the next day I start with my nose well and truly in front of the Grumbling Don, but as we all know it's never over until the fat one sings. In the end I had four winners at 5/2, 5/4, 9/4 and 7/1, which included the Derby winner, AUSTRALIA. I told him I was morally the winner last time with three winning days to his one, but this time there is no disputing who 'the man of the moment is.'

Better than the ego trip battle, is the fact that both my services are flying, as ANDY BELL actually made a 45 point profit yesterday, which puts us over the magic 100 points profit for the month, already, and not forgetting the LATE BETTING service which is just behind on 70ish points profit, so amazingly, as many of you are, if your part of both already we have profits of 180ish points.

Great times all round and while I enjoy people being successful at punting that doesn't always extend to the Grumbling Don and it was great to get one over on him. He didn't mention it afterwards though. Strange that….

Chapter 20

Beating the naysayers

I head to a two-day meeting at Yarmouth with The Machine riding shotgun. I see from the cards that it's going to be a day of favourites and tell my followers that though some of the prices are very short, they are still good things. Then I write:

A lovely sunny day again and there's plenty of flesh on show, a bit more than the Machine bargained for I am later told.

We are sitting outside the owners' and trainers' bar on the decking, when we are joined by a couple I know, whilst I am talking, I notice the Machine has put his sunglasses on and is talking to the lady of the party who's opposite him. I must admit she has very nice legs and her short skirt is showing them off to full effect. When they leave to go into the ring I find out why the Machine was very animated from behind his sunglasses, apparently her Lady Garden was in full view and the grass didn't need cutting. A winner already for the Machine hehehe.

The first day of racing was disappointing and day two passes without any more dramas or flashes of the Lady Garden so we head home. A quick pint in the Queen, while we wait for our Indian to be delivered. I'm jumping on the 8am rattler to York and what other idiot would have a Madras the night before a three hour train journey? I write:

Whilst I'm rattling towards York, I am told that Hannons' IVAWOOD is as good as their Hamdon winner at Newbury yesterday, knowing this I email him out and suggest filling our boots at 6/4. Ryan Moore looks an interesting booking for Roger Whitaker on LOVE ISLAND and I am also texted saying SOUVILLE is expected to win the last at Goodwood at 9/4.

I arrive in York at 11ish, with the Rock Holden waiting for me in his Oxfam suit and as I am walking from the station, as you can see on my Facebook page, I wonder if the Grumbling Don has finally emerged after getting beaten like a dog by me at Epsom.

With my tie firmly attached we arrive at the course and head upstairs to the owners' bar, where we watch Hughsey get us off to the best possible start by steering IVAWOOD to an easy and uncontested victory, today is already looking good and more importantly another winning one. Ryan Moore unfortunately can't maintain our great start and finishes third. A long wait now until we can hopefully cement our winning day. Luckily for the LATE BETTING SERVICE, the owners of SAVED BY THE BELL are in the bar and inform me that they don't think the 6lb rise is enough to stop him winning again, they agree to me sharing the information, as they have already had their monies on, so I complete my day and email this out.

The Rock breaks the seal on the first bottle of bubbly and it's now time to chill, we have both had good cash bets on SAVED BY THE BELL, which thankfully we can cheer home and collect our readies. A super day already and we can head into York knowing we have just one final piece of the jigsaw to complete.

Richard is his normal moaning self in The Waterfront and I am pleased to say the Tomahawk steaks are no more, after my moans last time and a nice sirloin and a Chablis are winging their way to our table four.

Oi oi SOUVILLE caps a great winning day for both services, as jointly we must have picked up nearly 30points profit.

I've not really mentioned it before but I do a regular slot for Betfan TV (www.betfan.com/tv) alongside Simon Holden and, I think, it's quite entertaining. It's certainly informative and I only mention it now because The Rock was very unhappy that I wouldn't give out any free tips for Royal Ascot. I'd done the work for my members so I wasn't planning on giving the tips away! Anyway, back in York, I write:

We leave for the races at 12ish, as I want to meet my good friend Michael Foulger, one of the Norwich City Football Club directors, who has two runners here today. All my bets are complete for the day, so it's a day for relaxing and enjoying the great racing on offer. We stop at the new bar on the main drag, near the arches, although it's very nice, it's a far cry from the strip club, Bohemia, it used to be.

As we are walking to the course, The Don takes great pleasure in giving us a beep as he passes. No Penny again, Simon and I wonder if there has been a stewards' inquiry on Bury Road, Newmarket, or maybe after the Don's beating maybe she has no new frock to wear.

We pop upstairs into the owners' and trainers' bar for a quick bottle of Heineken or two, as we have said we will be in the champagne bar, at 3ish to meet any BETFAN boys or girls that are here.

How close were we to absolutely cleaning up yesterday? I had three selections and all three ran good races. Katie Walsh couldn't quite get the old rogue SAPTAPARDI to put his head in front and was just beaten into a clear second by the Favourite, but secured our e/w money at the advised 11/2.

We get into the Champers bar early and luckily we do as we meet two great BETFAN lads and share the bottle with them. As it's time for NAADIRR to run the lads depart to get their monies on.

Even more heart breaking than the first was NAADIRR not quite getting up and losing by a nose at 14/1 and golly gosh it was my Saturday's column FREE tip as well as a private e/w service bet.

I seem to remember the Don's offer of a nice bottle of bubbly in his Sunday column, all I can say is I'm still waiting, I did give him a victorious smile when we did cross paths.

MON BRAV was our final bet in the last at 10/1 e/w and he was a fast finishing third, so 11/2, 14/1 and a 10/1 all placed, so we won money on all three of them, but it could easily have been so much better.

Never mind, we have made money again and I bet a lot of the crowd now leaving would swap. We head straight into town and as we have had a fair fill already, we decide to eat early as it's the England game later.

Once again we grace York's answer to dear old Floyd and take our usual seat in the back room at The Waterfront. Floyd, or better known as Richard, is very jovial and welcomes us with an Arkwright smile and a rub of his hands, obviously a 200 sovs last night smile. It's steak or steak boys, oh we have one salmon left, you just have to try it to believe it and for goodness sake get in there before 8pm. Surprisingly we both have a steak and the habitual bottle of red and white. As he has now ushered everybody else out he joins us with his own bottle and we have an in depth chat about tomorrow's runners, well Richard does and we listen, as it's his way or the highway.

Turns out I missed the England game too - too tired!

Sounds like I didn't miss much, the usual 'played well', 'need to improve' etc. I had two great days in York with a big profit and the winners keep on coming. By the middle of the month I have racked up a combined profit of more than 200 points. This activity must surely be hurting the 'greedy ones'?

Then I head to the first day of the fantastic Royal Ascot meeting with my fingers tightly crossed that I can continue my incredible run of form. Again, I've been caught on a good day and talked into offering a five day marathon for Betfan as a special service. Although I have my reservations about having to tip in every race for five days and attempting to make a profit because that's a big ask in anybody's book. So, obviously I agree to do it. I write:

TORONADO and KINGMAN are being touted as good things on day one and I have to agree, so I put both these out on the Ascot Special and also on ANDY BELL.

On ANDY BELL they are my only winners of the day and secures us a small day 1 profit. How impressive was KINGMAN? I certainly wouldn't be rushing to take him on if he turns up at Glorious Goodwood in the Sussex stakes. The Ascot special has also had these two winners and also HOT STREAK e/w, which finishes third, but unfortunately day 1 is a very small losing day to start the special.

Day 2 looks an impossible gambling day and if we come out of this with not only our shirts intact but also our pants we have had a right result.

On the ANDY BELL email I advise backing MUSTAJEEB at 11/2 e/w in the first, what on paper looks the day's banker TREVE and we will see how CERTIFY at 14/1 can perform without being filled with drugs after his year in rehab.

With all eyes on Ascot, I am reliably informed that we may be able to slip a couple under the radar at Ripon this evening. Not great prices, but I am told the connections will be very disappointed if they can't both oblige. As everything else is done I decide to put KICKBOXER at 6/4 and DUTCHBREEZE at evens up on THE LATE SERVICE as both win bets and also a larger win double.

MUSTAJEEB gets the special and also ANDY BELL off to dream starts, by winning nicely and limiting our possible losses. TREVE is very disappointing and trails in a well beaten third and CERTIFY flounders in last, obviously needing another jab or two to find his form, which had him as favourite for the Guineas.

I know hindsight and all that stuff, but after TREVES' race the trainer saying he didn't move well to post and Frankie saying he never felt right under him going to the start, shouldn't a vet or something have been involved? If a Formula One car doesn't go well on its warm up lap, it's straight into the pits, I know it's my pocket talking here and my clients.

Thanks to MUSTAJEEB we escape the impossible looking

day two with another small loss, I am aware I need to perform or these small loses will mount up.

After all the dramas of Ascot I nearly forget our two runners at what seems a lowly Ripon evening meeting. KICKBOXER and DUTCHBREEZE are both smashed off the boards and win very nicely for us and nets THE LATE BETTING SERVICE just under 30 points profit.

Day 3. Oi Oi both services are today over the magic 100 points profit mark for the month, ANDY BELL is on 135 and LATE BETTING has racked up 101 points and sitting top of the BETFAN tree in 1st and 2nd.

As I say in ANDY BELLS and the Specials emails I fancy today's racing as they look like my type of races.

Newmarket is not hearing of defeat for CANNOCK CHASE, so he appears as a Max bet at 9/4. Also on both services are TO BE DETERMINED at 10/1 and in the last WINDSHEAR at 5/1. On the special Ascot service only MISSUNITED at 50/1 available at 80/1 for the Gold Cup and HORS DE COMBAT at 14/1.

We bomb out badly in the first finishing 11th. CANNOCK CHASE is as good as we are told and gives Sir Michael and Ryan Moore their first winner of the week and kicks our day into profit. MISSUNITED has me shouting all the way down the home straight, I don't care about patriotism right at this moment and HRH and her ESTIMATE can finish an honourable second or third for all I care, silk bowlers lifted to MISSUNITED, she ran an absolute cracker and was only just beaten in the final strides and what a coup we would have had, if only, hey.

HORS DE COMBAT gets going too late and finishes third at 8/1 once again making our 12s look good and when Hughsey hits the front on WINDSHEAR I think it's job done, a nice 5/1 winner, only for King Kieran to cruise up and pass us leaving us a clear second.

As I have just said, although we have secured a nice profit on both the Special and ANDY BELL, it still leaves me thinking "if only."

Day 4. Again I like the look and the profile of today's Ascot card. Sir Michael is again attempting to get Her Majesty in the winner's enclosure with BOLD SNIPER, who I am reliably told has done a sparkling last piece of work with yesterday's winner CANNOCK CHASE and Gold Cup 2nd ESTIMATE, so this is my max for the day, working round him, I also put up ADELAIDE at 9/4, who on Saturday was only 2 lengths behind AUSTRALIA, I know that Roger Varion is very sweet on CURSORY GLANCE in the first at 16/1 and the very easy Yarmouth winner HORSTEAD KEYNES at 8/1 in the lucky last.

It's another great start as CURSORY GLANCE bolts home in the first at an advised 16/1 and gets yet another day off to a steaming start, that's three first race winners in the four days. HRH will have to wait as BOLD SNIPER finishes second, he doesn't look the easiest of rides either and I think Ryan Moore did really well. ADELAIDE is made to look ordinary by another Mr Gosden flying machine EAGLE TOP. This has St Ledger winner written all over it, but I fear Mr Gosden may take the NATHANAL route and go the King George route with him.

As I say we have to chuck a couple of points away in the 5.00 as I have to bet in every race and we do. Our hopes are pinned on Jamie Spencer and HORSTEAD KEYNES in the last, who we know can be quite brilliant or awful, hence his nick name Marmite, as you either love or hate him. You pays your money and take your chance is the old saying, we did, we knew what we were getting with Spencer on board, once again the best horse got beat and why, oh why did he have him so far back? I know that's his style, but ten lengths with only a furlong to go? That's rather extreme, surely, even as it's my/our pockets talking.

Once again I am left thinking, "if only."

Thankfully, I can say a rare losing day for ANDY BELL and the LATE BETTING SERVICE as combined we were killed by three seconds. It's not doom and gloom because both services combined are still well over the 200 points profit for the month, which should pay for your holidays and a few beers at a measly tenner a point that's well over two grand already this month.

Day 5. Oh no, I thought, here were go again, as we hit another 2nd in the first race with TOSCANINI at 11/2, making that six for the week and even worse when Mrs Cecil's HAMELIN was unsighted. Light was at the end of the tunnel as Sir Michael's ex-Derby hope TELESCOPE soon has us cheering our first winner of the day home at a great price of 9/4. Ryan Moore was supremely confident as he took it up 2f out and never looked like getting caught. We then backed Paul Hanagan to make amends for his poor Newmarket ride on ALJAMAAHEER and although he didn't quite get up again, I proportion no blame towards the jockey this time.

Once again we had a really good early start and I was conscious that the points and winnings were slipping away again and next we had the very difficult Wokingham. BACCARAT was our selection, as I thought his last run at York was very encouraging and the stable has always believed in his ability, at 14/1 he looked a cracking e/w bet, BACCARAT made his run up the stands rail and hit the front at the furlong post and pulled clear to win a very difficult looking Wokingham quite easily. Oi oi a 14/1 winner!

Our day finishes with two winners, two seconds and a non-runner in the last. So in all a very profitable last day and after the impossible looking task we were set of picking a horse in every one of the 30 races over five days, I am pleased to say and also proud, that we have finished about a cup of tea out.

In summary, we have finished the Royal Ascot special with at least one winner on every day, totalling an amazing seven for the meeting and not forgetting the dreaded and sometimes heart-breaking seven second places.

I wasn't at Ascot for the final day as I went to Newmarket for my corporate day. I actually quite like these events - they are fairly well paid, you get to meet some great people and there's plenty of food and drink on offer. For all of you doubters, I gave a very entertaining talk about what punters should look for when backing a winner.

I had put up Extortionist as my free column bet that day at 16/1, but had pre-warned all my own clients beforehand to grab the 16/1 as the price would collapse as soon as the email got out. I'd also had a very strong word from the all-conquering William Haggis stable regarding their Token of Love who was trading at 15/8. Having put Extortionist up as an e/w bet at 16/1 and Token of Love as a win bet at 15/8, I also decided to advise putting the two up in our once frowned upon e/w double. I write:

Newmarket is lovely today: the sun is shining and there is a spring in every non-footballing fan's step. With my chat done and tips advised, with the hospitality wine and food consumed, I can leave the box on the pretence of wanting to look at the paddock. Hehehe I pop in the owners' bar for a quick beer and a nose around. The art of this tipping game in corporate boxes is to earn your X's, have a drink and a bite to eat and leave before your fancied runners ply their trade. It's suicidal to remain in there, in case it all goes tits up and you have to endure all the sideways glances that cut you in half and the early day ladies, which are no more, wine-fuelled tongue lashings. I will get shot for letting out the real trade secrets, but you know Bellie Boy by now, no secrets here.

Oi oi Mr Haggis, you should be a Sir by now, as he bangs in our first winner, so NOW it's time 'just to pop' back and receive the smiles the 'well dones' and, of course, the now readily available bubbles and I smile to myself as I earwig the wives telling their men, that's why the Greedy 1s invite us, not because they like us, cause you don't listen and always lose, OMG, did I really write that and not just think it?

Back to the paddock and EXTORTIONIST looks bang on his game and is all the rage in the ring and has been punted into 8/1.

Get out Jim, don't get blocked in, he does and he doesn't and runs away with the race. I take a deep intake of breath as he passes me a length to the good and instead of the almighty Oi Oi, I walk back calmly and as cool as possible having just won a tad over £10k and just as importantly making over 150 points profit for all my loyal BETFAN clients.

NOW it really is time to 'pop back' and enjoy the plaudits, wine, bubbles and whatever their corporate expense account cards will stretch to.

Obviously there are no e/w doubles being claimed, as the ANDY BELL clients are about too, but after the rollicking the men have received after missing the first winner, thankfully most have backed EXTORTIONIST at around 10/1.

Thankfully, as I leave the box and wander down the avenue towards the exit, Colin, who has driven me is waiting and that is another very successful and extremely profitable day completed.

Sunday morning and it wasn't one of my better ideas to twist Colin's arm into stopping for a few on the way home, as this morning the hangover is much worse than the bank balance. We are miles out in front on the BETFAN who's who tree with an incredible 287 points profit for June already and certainly not forgetting the LATE SERVICE, who are sitting on 73 points profit, no "O" levels required to work out, sod the points, whatever your stakes, that's a serious amount of cash made by us all.

One thing I am very happy about is the profits have been gradually built up over the course of June and not in one lucky hit, when often it's on the back of a long losing run and all the punters are skint and have never got on, which is no use to man or beast.

Nice and early emails out today saying I am no good and couldn't tip rubbish, so I cry off and dread the pre-holiday shopping trip in to the city.

On the Monday I get a very excitable call. As you all now know, I love everybody winning and my very good friend and drinking partner 'Paul Cabbage' reveals that he also stung bet365 for just over £12,000 as well on our Super Saturday.

Chapter 21

Venting my anger. Again.

Honestly, when punting is good and as enjoyable as my day in Newmarket, there's no better way to live your life.

I think I could make a TV series called 'An Idiot Abroad'. I spend a lot of time in Malta so I'm used to sitting in cafes and bars watching the racing back home on my iPad (mind you, the family are also used to it too. Thankfully!). The clock is running down and I'm really keen to get the late service over the 100 points barrier.

In addition, I'm also pushing for my personal service to reach the magical 300 points mark. It would be a great result but when I'm in Malta I tend to overindulge and spend time relaxing and fishing and eating. This doesn't stop me from landing some good winners though I fail to reach 300 points. You would think that I'd be ecstatic with a result that sees me with 290+ points but no, I vent my anger on Facebook. Fortunately, a Dr Newland's ride romps for home to help the late service over the 100 point line.

Then on the Monday, the last day of the month, I have some very good news. I write:

I have achieved both my monthly goals as both our services have reached their targets, ANDY BELL has hit over 300 points and the LATE SERVICE over 100 points profit for the month and are sitting pretty at the VERY top of the table, where we have been for most of the month and also fourth, not bad for all you people in both services, hey?

I know and can confirm that three of my clients have booked super holidays around the world, thanks to our combined efforts, Australia, New York and Italy, if there are anymore of you lurking out there, I would love to know via BETFAN or my ANDY BELL RACING Facebook page.

Nice and early we get sorted on this last day of June, with a super strong word for HARWOODS STAR of Amanda Perritt's in the last at Windsor.

On ANDY BELL's service, I put it up as a 1 point win, as whatever happens we can then stay over the 300 points profit for the month, but in my appraisal, I tell all my clients that I am having more on, naughty I know. The LATE SERVICE also gets the same message.

The horse didn't win and after a heavy night out with friends, I'm alarmed to find after waking up that I've been engaged in a Facebook argument with the Tartan tipster. I have no recollection of it and going through the messages I can see it was all quite civil. I was cringing at some of my posts and even the big Betfan cheese SJM also got involved, thankfully I kept my more controversial views to myself even regarding the lack of height of Hadrain's Wall between us and there was nothing too offensive said. The only conclusion we ALL came to, and all agreed on, was that Simon Holden is a tart.

I'm left thinking that there could be an English vs Scottish challenge looming, so we can show us Brits have by far the best premier league of tipsters and do rule supreme. The issue of taking my iPad out with me doesn't come without problems. I write:

A winning day for both services yesterday and we have our month up and running. A busy day looms with three selections SWISS CROSS, FRANGIPANNI and ARABIAN REVOLUTION. With all three backed and emailed out, I also decide to put the three in an e/w trixie at 2/1, 13/8 and 2/1.

A shade later the Charlie Hills trained Gimcrack entrant, STRATH BURN is given to me as a very strong e/w bet at 13/2, although I know and also mention in my LATE SERVICE email the favourite is well thought of but it is of no value at around even money.

We have a meal booked at a very nice restaurant tonight and as our four runners are in the 7.10, 7.35, 8.10 and finally the

9.10, I take my iPad to watch their progress. In the middle of my prawn Bisque, I let out a squeak, to a few 'looks' - hot, hot I say, as SWISS CROSS just hangs on and wins at an incredible SP of 11/4. A distinct shout greets STRATH BURNs 7/1 clear win, a fish bone is my next excuse, father is smiling as he has also backed them all and knows the score. Unfortunately, I am unable to piss off the 'lookers' anymore, as the best the next two can muster is a second.

I know we have had a right result on the LATE SERVICE with a 7/1 winner and I think we may just have won on ANDY BELL, so another very satisfactory day's work complete.

I enjoy the next few days, the incredible Maltese hospitality and some fantastic fireworks, before writing:

A big week is looming, not only my long awaited return, but also the small matter of the fantastic July Cup, a three day meet, where, if like other years, we will clear up. Simon Holden has said he is going to grace us with his presence and I'm sure The Grumbling Don will be lurking, no doubt in his overcoat, maybe I will get my Bollinger! It's good being an honourable loser but not good talking the talk and then being a welsher, talking of Welshers, I wonder whether that Shrewd tipster aka Jimmy "Gordon Brooooooown" Welsh will hike down to watch some real racing.

After 14 days, it's time to come home. I've made 20+ points profits during my sunshine stint and then I'm straight into Newmarket for two days. As soon as I get back, Simon Holden comes to stay and says he is doing a special service for the three day July Cup meet. Good luck, I tell him, because he will need it with all the forecast rain. I write:

I head to the Newmarket July meeting and one of my favourites at this course, normally we do very well and win lots of money. I just hope the ground stays sound and has not been over watered.

I have arranged to pick up Mr Jolly and my father and treat them to some of the unique sights of Ladies' Day. Just as we hit the A14, I wonder whether I have made the correct decision with my two invitees, as it starts hammering down with rain.

If that's not bad enough we hit traffic just as we cross the traffic lights on to the Bury Road, still three or four miles from the course, as we pass Bedford lodge the first race is off, not a good start as I wanted to see how our Royal Ascot second WINDSHEAR runs.

We finally splash into the car park and OMG I'm not going to retract my earlier comments about "I hope the ground stays sound" because it hasn't and I am convinced we have already done a large amount of our hard-earned on Richard Hannon's, COULSTY before we even enter the course, as he doesn't want any cut at all.

Now, I am soaked, virtually lost my money and pissed off by constantly dodging and ducking umbrellas, Malta and her sunshine already seems a far cry away.

Simon is waiting for us, soaked standing under a tree and his tan suit looks like Captain Birdseye's waterproofs. With a grimace, as we are late, he greets us and we head to the owners' and trainers' bar.

What a shame. I so do feel sorry for all the girlies as it's absolutely pouring with rain and I am sure lots of them have been planning their outfits and day out for months.

The bars are all rammed as the rain doesn't stop and doesn't look like doing so and the day is spoilt for so many, even us as our COULSTY doesn't go a yard in the soft and, as I had feared, our monies are blown. The ground has certainly now gone and I am going to cut my stakes until things settle down again.

Day 2 of the July Cup. Although yesterday I said I was going to cut my stakes, the French filly HIGH CELEBRITY, has come into today's race with such a reputation, I just can't help myself and have a big bet on her and advise all of my clients to do likewise and take the 5/6 on offer. I am still very wary of the ground at Newmarket, so our next bet is at Ascot and it's the Mr Haggis trained ARABIAN COMET which is ridden by Jimmy Fortune and is trading at a tasty 6/1.

Manchester Pete arrives at my house at 11am and we set off for the course, Basil Holden should already be there as he stayed in

Cambridge last night, allegedly. Pete has booked us into what I think is the Rutland Arms on the High Street, so I tell Basil this and tell him he can crash in one of our rooms and get his work done until we arrive. Pete turns left at the clock tower, to my surprise as the Rutland is on the High Street and when we turn into the Heathcourt, I say to him I thought we were in the Rutland, no the Heathcourt, he says. I call Basil who has had a right stand-up row with the receptionist at the Rutland because she won't let him in our room as she has no knowledge of our booking! I wonder why? He is not best pleased when we tell him we are a mile up the road.

The weather is better, which is more than I can say about the Frenchman's ride on HIGH CELEBRITY, who, in his right mind gives Ryan Moore a four length start, a man who is riding like a demon at the moment? We finish a clear second, on the best horse, in my opinion and Ryan gives David Elsworth his day in the sun with a Group 1 winner, not literally.

Oi Oi Jimmy's not out of his ground on ARABIAN COMET as he wins very nicely at a well punted 9/4 and gives us over 20 points profit, but don't forget the Frenchman has chucked away a 10 point maximum which still leaves us with a very nice profit on the day.

I was made to have my semi-sensible head on by the more mature Manchester Pete and we had a nice meal in town, well OK-ish. We popped into The Yard to see if PCH was around and whilst we were there we lighted the Bin Suroor Indian boys' payroll by kicking their arses at pool. We moved into the High Street and popped in the White Hart, which was buzzing, Simon Basil Holden was in top form and using his best chat up lines, until I ruined it for him by asking his lady friends whether they were gypsies, as they didn't greet this with smiles and flutters we quickly left. Last port of call was The Kings club where Captain Bailey (the trainer Alan Bailey) normally plies his trade and we weren't disappointed as he was in great form. I/we had a right result as I made a great contact from a top Northern yard. I think our night ended at about 2.30am, so I think tomorrow may be a shade quieter, but who knows.

Day 3 Surprisingly it's an early rise, Basil has actually caught his 7am train to York and I am really up for today's JULY CUP, which is normally run at a blistering pace, I don't think there will be any track records broken in today's conditions. As yesterday, I think we will have lots of non-runners, which is far from ideal, especially when we are trying to obtain the best prices and value for us all early doors.

As is expected, the memories of my 300 points profit of a couple of weeks ago are now distant memories and I write in my diary about the flack I get from people because the service goes 18 points down in early July! There's no pleasing some people and some of the comments on my Facebook that question my abilities are simply hilarious! In fact, they are so good that I urge everyone to have a look at the moaners and whingers and keep in mind how much money they must have made a few short weeks ago. It's a funny old game!

Anyway, the July Cup was a great event, despite the weather. I racked up 30 points on the second day though I'm hoping it was the weather that put people off attending. I know some racecourses are seeing a decline attendance and I don't want this meeting to go the same way. It's a shame but then I did enjoy some decent winnings (as I usually do here) and me and Manchester Pete plunged £400 at 7/2 on ESTIDHKAAT and then £700 on WHEN WILL IT END at 2/1, which resulted in two happy chappies walking down the tree avenue towards the car. I write:

It's the World Cup final tonight and, to be honest, I have as much interest in watching that as I would in helping Simon "Basil" Holden pick some new suits. Old Donny Boy is still taking the Arthur Bliss, regarding the Bollinger, to be honest I don't give a flying, but it's good to name and shame.

Pete and I stop at the Wagon and Horses in the High Street, a great pub that was once run by a great friend and landlord. It used to be a real buzzing place and always packed, unfortunately the bank never got ANY of his takings, Greedy Joe Coral hovered up 99% of that.

My mate was one of the world's worst gamblers but also one of the world's nicest blokes and the story goes, because thankfully I wasn't present, that he had got in well over his head and borrowed a very large sum of money and not kept up the repayments. Unfortunately, the lenders were not as lenient as Barclays and took him for a drive to a quiet little place to sort this oversight, shall we say, out. Talk about taking the bull by the horns, in his most fluent Irish accent as soon as he was ushered out of the car, he said, "Do me a right fucking favour, now, shoot me, right here." I don't know what the resolution was and don't want to, all I can tell you is my great friend is still here to tell the story, albeit not in the Wagon any more.

We leave the Wagon for another of his ex-haunts, the Kentford Cock and true to form Joe Coral ruined this place as well. It's also not half the place it was, although I don't think the VAT and taxmen will agree.

We get to our final port of call, nice and close to home, The Swan, where we discuss and analyse three varying days at the July Course over a couple of lovely bottles of Chateau Neuf De Pape and a good steak.

Pete has left mine by the time I rise at 7am on his four hour journey back up the M14 and M6. I hear the final was as dull as Basil's suits, so we didn't miss much. Today's racing looks just as dull, but I do manage to find three selections and email them out.

For the sake of continuity, I'll reprint what else I said:

Not much happening today, too wet to grass cut, the system is close to overload, so I plan a couch day, only to be scuppered by demands to go out for lunch, which after three days of, not all work, I can hardly refuse.

I arrive home, after a nice lunch, to see both my horses have been beaten and a non-runner, incredibly there are comments on Facebook regarding the two losses, amazing creatures some gamblers! We have won over 30 points in the last three days, at a very difficult July Cup meeting, over 300 points last month, well over 500 points this year and anybody would think that two losers today is the end of creation! Well, I really don't know but I just smile and think tomorrow is another day.

A couple of days, and a few decent winners, later, I write about going to a night meeting at Yarmouth. The card consists of small fields and the look of most favourites winning.

The trip to Yarmouth is going without any great dramas, until I am halfway there and get a call saying not to forget we are booked into The Suffolk Hotel tonight. Oh crap, I don't let on that I had totally forgotten and have brought absolutely nothing with me for the overnight stay! Oh well, I can't let them down and there are plenty of shops along Regent Road, where I can soon buy some undies and smellies in the morning.

Yarmouth is quiet again tonight, I just wonder whether Arena Leisure are pulling a fast one by shutting the doors in early September for 'remedial' work to the track and allegedly re-opening next June. Now all you Dick Francis readers, what about if a bomb is found under the track, or a mine shaft or sand subsidence or Martians landed and it couldn't reopen, oh what a shame! Arena Leisure are left with the headache of marketing a multi-million pound house building project. Mmmmmm maybe and hopefully not, you read it here first.

Anyway, I find a decent double that should return more than 160 points but I get let down with a poor result. I'm so despondent that I head home and ignore the text messages from those I was meant to be having a night out with. Most do not need to be repeated. For some reason I just can't get going this month; I have a good winning day and a bad losing one. I know my network of contacts will come good for me.

I head to Doncaster for an evening meet and after a quick freshen up in the hotel find the track is very quiet. That is until Captain Bailey and his crew walk into the owners' and trainers'. With his habitual pink bubbly and a wry smile, he and his mob join me at my table and I think things could possibly get out of hand in a very short time. Thankfully, I have a good win and pick up a big wedge from a William Hill rails bookie, who was less than happy at handing over the money, and I write:

The bubbles are now freely flowing and the Captain is in top form and the charisma of this 75 year old gentleman trainer always seem to attract a predominantly female crowd, which isn't a bad thing as a dark haired beauty stands out and The Greyhound Master would have been in his element as one of the ladies in our party is a lady who trains 150 greyhounds, what a looker! If this is what all lady greyhound trainers look like I may jump ship! She has given us what she thinks is a good thing for next week so I shall include him in my email for all that are interested.

We are the last to leave the owners' bar and I am thankful that I have a hotel booked as all the Newmarket boys are moaning that the A1 is closed and they have a five hour drive to look forward to.

The next day I wake up with the dark beauty on one side and Greyhound Ruth on the other, oh OK in my dreams. Reality is that my head is banging and I have to be on my toes as I am catching the 9.17 train out of Donny and heading to Newmarket for tonight's racing and not forgetting the Beach Boys, who are performing after racing, who I shall not be staying for, I hasten to add.

An incredibly busy day and I have five very live horses that we need to be backing, luckily I have a forty five minute wait at Cambridge and with the Cloud wifi I can get everything emailed out.

I have arranged to meet a trainer's head lad and also the main work rider for the Boys in Blue in the Wagon. I want to add these two to my already strong flat racing portfolio if I can.

This afternoon's office is the Wagon and we have a few beers whilst watching the racing, beats most offices I bet. The deal is done and we have two great new contacts that we can rely on and the Boys in Blue have a maximum nap next week to kick us off with.

We get to Newmarket nice and early as the track will be full of flowery shirts and straw hats tonight to cheer on the Beach Boys.

Captain Bailey looks none the worse for our Donny exploits and jockey's agent Paul is his normal reserved self. The racing is OK but nothing special and our Mr Haggis horse which had apparently come on a stone since last year is rubbish and looks to have regressed.

Chapter 22

The finishing line looms...

It's another Saturday and as the card is already difficult to work through I'm put out that there has been a huge thunder and lightning storm which will affect racing in my part of the country. More importantly, it will affect me more because lightning struck our pole and knocked out the internet and phones. I manage to get round the problem but it just adds to the issues of meeting an early deadline.

I know that I drive myself and my members bonkers when I fail to find the winners - I confess that I need to shape up and attempt to bang in some winners before the month ends. I write:

Steve is very joyous as he informs me that the good Doctor's HEWDYERWHEESHT is expected to run a big race today at 10/1. He also tells me that MAZ WARD at 12/1 and CREEVYTENNANT at 8/1 are also not out of things, so I decide to back and email all three out as a big priced e/w trixie.

I am also given PROFESSOR who runs at Haydock tonight and is trading at 5/2 as a very strong bet and I am informed his homework has been scintillating. As I attempted to be too clever for my own good last week, with my free column tip, by putting up a

50/1 shot, which lost, I want to make amends, so I put up PROFESSOR as a very strong free column bet advising all to take the 5/2, this also goes out to all my clients.

I get Tom and Pete to also put ARTFUL PRINCE in an e/w double with PROFESSOR for me and this completes my bets and emails for the day. I pick the Great Alfonze up from The Inn and we head towards Newmarket.

We arrive in good time, he can't wait to give John Christie, the best rails bookmaker, some of his hard-earned and proceeds to the ring. As I am not intending to have a punt at Newmarket, I settle outside the owners' and trainers' bar, which overlooks the pre-parade ring.

It's a fantastic day, the sun is shining and I think it would be very difficult to find a better office than this.

The good Doctor punts his and we just miss out on a place, annoyingly 4th. MAX WARD runs a cracking race at 12/1 and finishes 2nd, so a small profit. For a horse that is not certain to stay I find the forcing tactics on CREEVYTENNANT very bizarre and, sure enough, he fades away into the distance, maybe they have another day in mind, where he will be dropped in trip or ridden more conservatively.

Alfonze, with his face blood red, steams in with the first two winners at Newmarket under his belt and complains that the wine effects his gout and gets a pint. I receive a phone call from some of our local girls, thinking they just want some Saturday tips and I am pleasantly surprised to hear they are in fact here and on a 21st jolly up.

We immediately leave our wine in Michael's capable hands and head to the champagne tent, near the winning line. With silly flower necklaces round their necks, their faces are a similar colour to the Alfonze's, but I suspect it is alcohol induced rather than blood pressure. Sure enough they are already steaming, Tina who's my age, is the leader and in her bestest girlie voice mentions she has never tried a bottle with the orange label. How can you refuse, what's now fourteen pairs of cow eyes staring at you? Simple, you can't, although saying that the Alfonze's mobile did mysteriously ring at that precise moment. £71 lighter and I am left thinking maybe I have been groomed, hopefully all in a good cause.

The bottle just about manages a full circuit and I'm on my toes back to the trainers' bar, with Tina and Claire the teacher in tow, oh yes and old red face bringing up the rear.

The wine has evaporated, down Mike's throat I think, and the Alfonze sees the opportunity to get a round in, with no orange labels in sight, I hasten to add. Tina backs her first winner and Alfonze wins his third and all is well. Even better when Mr Bailey joins us with his pink bubbles. I'm not so sure it was my presence that prized him out of the bar, but even money it was the teacher's ample thighs on show. She is now struggling and couldn't correctly mark pre-school exam papers, certainly not perturbed by this, Captain Bailey is full on and I hope teacher has hopefully got her cane concealed somewhere as protection as some naughty thoughts and stories are being played out in certain minds.

How do these women do it? Tina backs her 2nd then 3rd, because it wears a hood and looks like batman and fourth, because it had a crap and must be lighter, winners. Teach has her eyes and thighs shut, so the Captain retires to his mates in the bar.

The girls go back to the party a lot fuller than when they left and it's just me and Alfonze left. As he has only had a couple of pints he offers to drive and we head home with the PROFESSOR to look forward to.

Professor was a good winner for us, a great result because I also gave it as a free tip. There are no bets on that Sunday and I chill out and recharge my batteries. On the Monday I'm on the road at 5am and heading towards Newmarket, as I want to watch one particular horse in the first string on the racecourse side gallop. I already know that if this training session goes well he will be entered into a relatively easy looking race on Friday and I will be having a very big punt on him. I write:

After the gallops we stop at the White Lion for some breakfast and whilst there I am told that everybody expects SHARMAS SONG of Sir Michael's to be responsible for getting

Ryan Moore to the 100 winners for the season. With this emailed out and bet, I head for home.

On the way, I get a huge word for FACTOR FIFTY, who at 14/1 I am told is a huge price and now back on good to firm ground is a must bet. With IRENE HULL and BALLYBORGH GORTA all my bets and emails are complete.

I have to book my hotels and trains for the end of the week as the plan, at the moment is, to go up to Doncaster on Thursday to back the winning machine from the Chris Wall stable, SYRIAN PEARL and then on to York for the Friday night and Saturday day meets.

FACTOR FIFTY runs a huge race at a smashed up 9/2 and again finishes second, with our 14/1 banked we make a nice profit, but nothing like a win would have paid.

IRENE HULL runs well below par and thankfully BALLBOROUGH GORTA gets in the winner's enclosure for the LATE BETTING SERVICE.

This run of seconds is starting to get to me - it's the reason why the points aren't clocking up on the Betfan board. I've managed at least 12 this month, nowhere near good enough for someone at my level. Although this is most annoying, it does show the information and form readings are the same and I'm just not getting the rub of the green at the moment. If only 10%-15% of the seconds had won, I would be bang up there again. It's so frustrating! However, I have a good trip for the Yorkshire circuits planned and I write:

I leave nice and early to catch the 2.11pm rattler up north for tonight's racing at Doncaster. The main reason for the trip is to back the Chris Wall trained SYRIAN PEARL, who is in flying form at home and is expected to win. I also email out ALONSOA at 11/8, MARSALI at 11/4, GLOBAL LADY at 6/5 and finally BEACH OF FALESA also at 11/4.

I will have to let the two elderly statesmen, my father and Mr Jolly make their own way to Great Yarmouth today.

Basil Holden in his column today says he dresses like George Clooney, lol, more like George Roper.

ALONSOA gets our day off to the best possible start by winning and then it gets even better with a power packed ride by Ryan Moore on GLOBAL LEADER. Two winners and my main bet hasn't even run yet. BEECH OF FALESA is added to our ever growing second list after looking like the winner.

MARSALI runs as if there is something amiss. SYRIAN PEARL appears to get up bang on the line and has me doing a jig as I have had a huge win bet at 7/2 and with best odds guaranteed I have copped the 6/1 sp. Betfair backs up my view as he is trading at 10/1 ON and the cameraman also agrees as he is the horse in view.

Bang, doom and gloom as number 7 is called the winner, although I watch another five or six reruns and still think we have won, there's no big pay-out for Bellie Boy on this occasion. Absolutely gutted with the 13 seconds now for this month, I leave for some comfort food.

Once again the Chinese that finished off the evening was spot on, a quick taxi back to the hotel. Why me, is what I say, 365 days a year the hotel porter has to shag the night receptionist and tonight he couldn't keep it in his pants. After five minutes of ringing the bell and no answer, full of wine Bellie Boy decides the only way in is through the security window. These windows, as you know only open so far, so you can imagine trying to prise my ample bulk through was not easy, thankfully a chair was just under the window for me to fall on with a bang as it toppled over, just as a very flustered looking receptionist reappeared and a smirking porter, the key was quickly given and I retired after another eventful day.

Early up, past a grinning day receptionist and across to Asda to get the RP. On my return to the hotel I am greeted with giggles and morning Charles? Why Charles, I question the now laughing receptionist? Well I thought you were Charles Pearce, still I haven't cottoned on. Charles Pearce the famous cat burglar she says, I now have a rough idea where she is coming from, but I'm amazed the night receptionist has mentioned my antics, because of hers, she hadn't, look here she says, pointing at her computer screen, in full view of the security cameras, which is now showing on her screen is me prising myself through this half open window and very gracefully crashing over the chair. It was very funny. Only Andy Bell.

I am catching the 2.11 train from Donny to York and meeting Basil Holden at the station. As usual he is late and I can't believe I have asked Roper the fashion icon to bring me a tie as I haven't packed one, as usual, as I hate wearing them. Basil brings me a garish stripy purple tie, but hey, beggars can't be choosers.

MADE IN RIO makes my Stella taste a shade sweeter as he wins nicely and we have made the perfect start. Next EURO CHARLINE bolts in and we are already sitting pretty with two bets and two winners.

Eddie the stat, meets us with his entourage for a pre-race beer. As we are walking to the course he suddenly turns right to the County stand, or the cheaper end, hehehe maybe he should try and be a good tipster and not the Betfan tea boy.

I head straight for the TVs to watch Ascot and to my horror and dismay, I can't believe mid-July and it's absolutely chucking it down, which will certainly not suit our next two runners.

CHARLES CAMOIN doesn't go a yard on the softened ground and I have major fears for our bet, GABBIANO in the last.

After hitting 1.8 in running and looking the most likely winner, GABBIANO's finish is blunted by the ground and what started off as a super day has fizzled out due to the rain. As if my luck isn't bad enough this month with 14 seconds in mid-July I am beaten by rain.

With my day ruined, I am in no mood to stay at the course to listen to the Beach Boys, so it's the early train back to Donny and hoping the night porter has already done his business. A change of plan this morning; I have binned York and I am heading homewards and to Newmarket to bet two runners there today as I have huge words for both.

I decide to take my dad racing at Newmarket and write:

My father and I arrive at Newmarket, it's a lovely sunny day and relatively busy. With all my bets complete, I pitch up in the owners' and trainers' bar, while my father goes to back both my selections.

The first shock of the day, and we haven't even had a race yet, is that Captain Bailey joins me at my table with a cup of tea. Mick the Fish, who is a Newmarket tipster and Trigger also join me. We have a bottle of wine and the Fish tells me he has had a huge word for Godolphin's other runner in our race and has got all his punters and himself on. I do tell him what I've heard as I hate people losing, but he sticks to his guns, which is fair enough.

Hitting the hill there is only one winner and thankfully for us it is FIRST FLIGHT and while the Fish's selection has veered towards Cambridge, we win easily. Fantastic start and we could have much more to come.

FAST TRACK hits the front two out and looks the most likely winner, his stride is shortening and as they flash over the line, I am gutted as I think we have been done and our wretched luck continues, as I sit down thinking if only, No 13 FAST TRACK is called the winner, I jump up and shout as if a wasp has just stung me on the arse and do a Clive Briton winning jig. My head is in a spin with loads of thoughts and figures, I can't quite believe what an amazing day all my clients and myself have just had, my father rushes in clutching his winning tickets, like a kiddie with an ice cream and joins our joyous table.

Both these tips were also in my last week's Saturday column, so I hope many of the 35,000 Betfan readers have also had it right off. Personally, I have had a cracking day and I am sure both Tom and Keith, my bettors have also.

The long and short is that every one of my clients has won well over 100 times their personal stakes, the column readers have had two great winners and I can now eat and drink well for the rest of the year.

I think this quote below is brilliant and was posted Saturday evening, by one of my clients, Ben Benji, after he had made a few scathing remarks and attacks on me, after, what, can I say, not our best two weeks and then just after our Super Saturday 100ish point win.

Mr Andy Bell: An apology.

"Over the last few days I may have created the impression that Andy Bell is a fat, drunken, loutish imbecile who should have been kicked out of Betfan Towers before the weekend's racing began.

"It has now come to my attention that he is in fact a racing wizard capable of emptying the Greedy 1's satchels single-handedly.

"I would like to apologise therefore to Mr Bell for any distress my earlier comments may have caused him and send the following message:

"Go get 'em Bellie Boy, you little Suffolkshire Star!"

Before I realised this was a rehash of what the Daily Mirror had said to Gazza prior, and after his wonder goal against Scotland in the Euro's, I did think that's a bit harsh to Bellie Boy, but very true, although I did think the fat bit was a bit debatable.

Obviously, with such a good winning day under our belts we hit Newmarket in grand style that night. I'm relieved because I'm now back on top of the Betfan tree with over 100 points profit and well clear of the Fixer. Without the fifteen seconds, it's frightening to think what a huge, huge profit we could have been sitting on.

It's a real shame that the 30+ people that left my service in this barren spell didn't have a little more patience and confidence in me. I genuinely mean that because I get a huge buzz out of knowing we are all winners and winning, making all the family and people around us happy and hated by the Greedy 1s.

I can't quite see how I can top the Newmarket result but life and work must continue. Over the coming days I rack up more points, one day it is 11 points and that disappoints me but two weeks previously I would have been really chuffed with that tally!

I must say, it's incredible isn't it how quickly the tide can turn? The last two weeks have been a nightmare, with all the hard luck stories and the 15 seconds and now, with what appears to be a click of the fingers, we bang in winner after winner! Now I'm merrily sailing along in the No 1 position as if nothing had ever happened, very bizarre and mind blowing this game.

Anyway, remember me meeting that greyhound trainer, the gorgeous one? Her tip was put out to my followers. It was called Exocet and it ran at Hove so I mark it up as an eight point win and snap up the 2/1 from William Hill. Needless to say, Exocet comes out of trap 6 like a missile and was never in any danger of losing. I was incredibly pleased that a dog had made my night – it's not often that I get to say that!

The run-in to the end of the month, and the end of my first year as a tipster with Betfan, is amazing. After 18, YES 18, seconds and a few hard luck stories, I completely turned things around after what looked like it was going to be a big losing month but by hitting an amazing SIX winning days on the trot, I finished well in profit with an incredible 130 points.

That was my Andy Bell service, the late service didn't fare as well but for anyone who is punting £20 a point, they have won a cool £2,600 tax free. Goodness knows what the braver members may have made but whatever it is - Oi Oi, just think of Bellie Boy when you spend, spend, spend.

It's been a great year working with Betfan and I'm dead set on winning even more in my second year. I'm proud of what I do, OK it's not a 'normal' career in most peoples' eyes but it is something I'm very good at and it's something I enjoy. I've made fantastic lifelong friends from travelling to the country's racecourses, I've had incredible days and downright horrible days but they have all been part of an incredible journey. So, let me leave you with one of my (many) sayings:

Never let the regrets in life be the chances you never took.

Andrew Bell

Printed in Great Britain
by Amazon.co.uk, Ltd.,
Marston Gate.